BY THE EDITORS OF
CONSUMER GUIDE®

CORVETTE
PAST · PRESENT · FUTURE

BEEKMAN HOUSE
New York

Manufactured in the United States of America
1 2 3 4 5 6 7 8 9 10

Library of Congress Catalog Card Number: 80-85365
ISBN: 0-517-359871

This edition published by:
Beekman House
Distributed by Crown Publishers, Inc.
One Park Avenue
New York, New York 10016

Contents

Corvettes
of the Past...page 6

A lively review of the Corvette's first 30 years—from its origins as a Motorama show car, through its near-demise, to its resurgence as "America's Only True Sports Car." From 1953's "plastic bathtub" to 1963's stunning Sting Ray, from the hot fuel-injected '57 to the big-inch 'Vettes of the early '70s, plus the glamorous show cars.

Corvettes
of the Present...page 52

The 1980-82 models not only maintain the tradition of style and stamina that has made Corvette a legend in its own time, but also give a tantalizing hint of what lies ahead. Here's a rundown on the Corvettes of the '80s, including the commemorative Collector Edition model, the last and best of the "big" 'Vettes.

Corvettes
of the Future...page 60

What will tomorrow's Corvettes be like? Here's a full description and drawings of the totally redesigned 1983 model—the most exciting 'Vette yet! Then, we take Corvette design concepts ahead by at least a generation in an intriguing series of design studies—from mid-engine GTs to a wild battery-powered Corvette of the 21st Century!

"Corvettes of the Past" was written by noted automotive historian Richard M. Langworth. Contributing author Mike McCarville supplied material for "Corvettes of the Present" and "Corvettes of the Future." Renderings of the 1983 Corvette and Corvette concept cars were conceived by well-known automotive illustrator Harry Bradley.

Special thanks to those individuals and organizations who provided invaluable photographic and research assistance, without which this book would not be possible: Charles M. (Chuck) Jordan, Director of Design, GM Design Staff, and Floyd Joliet, Administrative Operations, GM Design Staff (show cars and experimentals); Suzanne Kane, Ralph Kramer, Kay Ward, and Jim Williams, Chevrolet Motor Division Public Relations Department (production models and Bowling Green assembly plant); Geri Brehm and the staff at GM Photographic (production models); Becky Bodnar, *Corvette News* magazine; Trigger Alpert (1957 Corvette hardtop, color section); David Gooley (1955 Corvette, color section); and Richard M. Langworth (miscellaneous black-and-white photography).

Corvettes of the Past

The Chevrolet Corvette was born on June 30, 1953, when the first production model rolled off a short assembly line in Flint, Michigan. That first car represented several years of thought and months of frantic planning. Little did those who helped build that car realize they were giving birth to a legend. And if the Corvette can be said to have parents, they must surely be Ed Cole and Harley Earl.

Cole was the dynamo who came to manage Chevrolet Division in 1953, and almost single-handedly changed the make's image overnight. Born on a farm in Marne, Michigan in 1909, Cole had always been interested in things mechanical. Entering the GM Institute, he took part in a work-study program affiliated with Cadillac, and in 1933 was hired by that division as a full-time engineer. Before and during World War II, he designed Army light tanks, combat vehicles, and a new engine for the M-3 tank. Following the war, Cole temporarily involved himself with rear-engine prototypes for both Chevrolet and Cadillac. Soon, he was concentrating on engine work with Cadillac's John Gordon, and together they came up with the significant short-stroke Cadillac V-8 of 1949. Following a 30-month spell as manager of the Cadillac Cleveland plant, he came to Chevrolet.

"Chevy," Cole once said, "was an outfit you couldn't get your arms around." He became chief engineer in April 1952, and immediately enlarged the engineering staff from 850 to 2900. With this team he forged the milestone 265 V-8, introduced for 1955, followed by the legendary 283. He became division general manager in July 1956, and was elected a GM vice-president. He

Above: Factory "phantom" view reveals the 1953 Corvette's chassis layout. Heavy six was put well back for better weight distribution. Top: The Motorama show car, photographed in Europe. Right: Corvette project was cloaked by code name "Opel."

would later become the company's president.

"To lengthen and lower the American automobile, at times in reality and always at least in appearance," was the way Harley J. Earl summed up his work during his 31 years at General Motors. He arrived in 1927, preceded by a four-star recommendation, to

5

design the new LaSalle for
Cadillac. From then on he
dominated GM design. Earl's Art
and Colour Studio was the first
major recognition by a Detroit
manufacturer that a car's
appearance was as important as
its performance. In the Corvette
story, Harley Earl's role is vital, his
contribution enormous.

Earl was born to the trade. His
father had designed horse-drawn
carriages in Los Angeles. Young
Harley was a devotee of the
automobile by the time he was out
of Stanford. In the early '20s he won

fame as the designer of dashing
custom bodies for Don Lee, then a
doyen among Hollywood
coachbuilders. At Lee's he was
"discovered" by Lawrence P. Fisher
of Cadillac. Fisher recommended
Earl to GM president Alfred P. Sloan
Jr., and Harley signed on at age 32.

Art and Colour was Earl's
invention. He realized that one
man alone couldn't hope to carry
on the titanic design mission of
General Motors. He surrounded
himself with talented designers,
and many stylists owed their
careers to him. Virgil Exner, later to

win fame with the "Forward Look"
Chrysler products, trained under
Earl, and headed the Pontiac
studio in the 1930s. Frank Hershey,
Art Ross, Ned Nickles, and Bill
Mitchell made their own marks at
Cadillac and Buick. Clare
MacKichan, father of the '55 Chevy
design, was an Earl trainee.
Mitchell, of course, went on to
become Earl's successor, and had
an equally outstanding career.

Earl's imagination was tempered
by a shrewd understanding of
public taste, honed at countless
Motoramas and public showings.

Left: Contemporary factory photo shows the anatomy of the '53 Corvette body. Top: EX-122, the Motorama show car, poses with a stock 1953 Bel Air sedan. The difference in height is dramatic. Above: Job One comes off the Flint assembly line. Note stock Bel Air wheel covers.

"We can't afford big mistakes and we don't like little ones." The whole GM corporate philosophy is reflected in those few words. It is the reason the first Corvette was as good as it was, and the reason its successors steadily became better. Combined with the engineering expertise and enthusiasm of engineer Cole, the first Corvette could scarcely have had better parentage.

There wasn't much to work with for the first Corvette. The decision to build a sports car, at least as a Motorama showpiece, was taken in 1952. Cole had not yet begun to shake his staff by its collective scruff, and time was short. Most of the new car's mechanical pieces would have to be taken from Chevy's parts shelf, and they hardly promised excitement. This included the tried and true—but ordinary and slow—Blue Flame six.

None of this daunted Harley Earl. The success of Glasspar and the body-building potential of glass-reinforced plastic immediately attracted his attention. When he suggested GRP for a General Motors sports car, his superiors were enthusiastic. If GRP could work in a two-seater, they reasoned, it might work in larger cars.

Corvette development began in earnest in early 1952 with two separate efforts. The first was a conventional Chevrolet convertible built with a GRP body for testing purposes. The second was development of a chassis suitable for a GRP two-seater. The body testing proved highly satisfactory. A proving grounds driver unexpectedly rolled the car at high speed, and escaped virtually unhurt. Encouraged by what he saw, Earl commissioned a plastic two-seat roadster show car that would lead to the production Corvette.

The Corvette's styling expressed contemporary themes favored by the Art and Colour staff: wraparound windshield, pushbutton door handles, nerf-type bumpers, and metal top cover. There were chrome-plated mesh stone guards, used as much to protect the sunken headlamps as to add flavor to the front end. The toothy grille was a natural for the '50s, and later became the darling of customizers, who stuck it onto everything from big Chevys to Kaisers. Clean-lined and ground-hugging, the Corvette had the "wasp waist" look that fascinated Earl in those years, its beltline dipping aft of the doors before rolling back toward pointed taillamps and rounded rear fenders.

The styling job was completed in remarkably short order. Slim lead time, however, combined with budgetary considerations to make use of production components a must. Young Bob McLean laid out the chassis, starting, unnaturally, from the rear. He placed the seats ahead of a stock Chevy rear axle, then moved the engine and transmission as far back as possible to improve weight distribution, aiming for a 50/50 split front to rear. The drivetrain was also lowered for a lower center of gravity. Wheelbase was pegged at

Art & Colour Studio chief Harley Earl

102 inches, apparently because this was the same as that of the Jaguar XK-120, one of Earl's "benchmark" cars.

Predictably, power for the new car would be supplied by the 235-cubic inch Blue Flame six, then delivering 105 horsepower. For the Corvette, however, it was modified by fitting a high-lift long-duration camshaft, hydraulic valve lifters, and a high-compression head, all of which brought power up considerably. Three Carter type YH sidedraft carbs mounted on a special aluminum manifold did the rest. Result: 150 bhp at 4500 rpm. Chevy didn't have a manual transmission at the time suitable for an engine of this power, so engineers substituted two-speed Powerglide automatic, with revised shift points for more sporting response. This decision would later prove controversial.

The Corvette's suspension was of Chevy design and boringly conventional, but spring rates, shock settings, and ride stabilizer were all calibrated to suit a sporting car. Likewise, the Saginaw steering was a stock GM component, but had a much quicker 16:1 ratio. And the Corvette's steering wheel was an inch smaller in diameter than that of Chevy passenger cars.

While engineers labored with production development, Harley Earl and company were busy finalizing the Motorama show car, which would be a final test of public reaction to the design. With the exception of cowl-mounted fresh air scoops (which reappeared in non-functional form for 1956-57), the Motorama Corvette was one of the few show cars that went into production with its styling virtually intact. That Art and Colour's original design was retained, unsullied by committee modifications, enhances the appeal of early Corvettes among collectors today. There were dozens of detail differences, of course, between the Motorama car and the production '53. Underhood features eliminated for production included much chrome plating, a shrouded fan, and pancake-type air cleaners. "Corvette" script at front and rear was also deleted.

Features unique to the new sports roadster included its easy folding, manually operated fabric top, which disappeared into a covered compartment behind the twin bucket seats. Another first was the top's chrome-edged, removable, Plexiglas side curtains with push-pull vent wings. The Motorama car had exterior pushbutton door handles similar to those of the 1951 experimental Buick LeSabre, but they didn't make production. To open the Corvette's door, you thrust a hand through an open vent wing and slid the interior door release rearward.

The gleaming Polo White show car, with its bright Sportsman Red interior, was a hands-down success at the 1953 Motorama. Chevrolet

The production Corvette emerged with the original Motorama design virtually intact.

Above: A Corvette cavalcade rounds the infamous S-curve on Chicago's Lake Shore Drive. This was one of several 1954 publicity shots released to convince the public that Corvette production was fully underway at St. Louis. Left: These Corvette-based dream cars appeared at the 1954 Motorama. Shown are the fastback "Corvair," the Nomad wagon, and a prototype hardtop that appeared for '56. Below: The tricky-to-tune triple-carb "Blue Flame Six."

was soon inundated by inquiries. When would it be produced, and how much would it cost? It is apparent from drawings and dates that production was never doubted by Harley Earl and Ed Cole. Neither was there much debate between Chevrolet general manager Thomas Keating and GM president Harlow Curtice. The Chevrolet Corvette would go into production at the earliest possible date. Price was $3513.

The 300 Corvettes built for the 1953 model year were essentially handmade pilot units. Frames were supplied by a non-GM source, and the engines came from Chevy's engine plant in Tonawanda, New York. The body components — 46 separate pieces—were produced by the Molded Fiber Glass Body Company at Ashtabula, Ohio, and were glued together using wooden jigs. These early production cars showed considerable improvision. The first 25, for example, used stock Bel Air wheel covers. To simplify assembly and parts inventory, all '53s were finished in Polo White, with red and white interiors and black tops. All were equipped with 6.70 × 15 whitewall tires, Delco signal-seeking radio, and recirculating hot water heater. The instrument panel included a clock and a 5000-rpm tachometer. The mesh headlight guards and the clear Plexiglas cover that protected the rear license plate were both illegal in some states, so the owner's manual included instructions for their removal.

Rare and desirable today, the 1953 'Vette was considered something less than wonderful when new. Its typical 0-60 mph time was 11 seconds, and top speed was about 105 mph — not bad for 1953, but hardly in keeping with the state of the sports car art even then. The verdict from those schooled in the European tradition of sports cars was predictable: they didn't like it. They turned up their noses at the fake knock-off wheel covers, "rocketship" taillights, and that two-speed automatic. Nevertheless, the Corvette was a hit with dealers, who flooded

Chevrolet with orders. But the division had decided the first 300 Corvettes would be reserved mainly for dealers to lend out to local celebrities and prominent business or civic leaders for reaction and evaluation.

For the 1954 model year, Corvette assembly was moved to St. Louis, Missouri, where it would remain until 1981. By the middle of the calendar year, more than 50 cars per day were coming off the line.

Few significant changes were made for the '54s, but running alterations took place through the model year. Tops and top irons were changed from black to tan, and gas and brake lines were relocated inboard of the righthand main frame rail. The engine carried a new-style rocker arm cover, the wiring harness was cleaned up, and more plastic-insulated wire replaced the fabric variety. Engines, still built at Flint, were suffixed F54YG. This was also the first year a choice of colors

became available (approximate percentages noted in parentheses): Pennant Blue metallic (16) with tan interior, Sportsman Red (4) with red and white interior, and the usual Polo White (80) with red interior. A very small number, as few as six, were painted black, and also carried the red interior. Model year production totalled 3640 units.

The 1953 model had carried two short stainless steel exhaust extensions, exiting the body inboard of the rear fenders. It was soon discovered that air turbulence sucked exhaust fumes back against the car, soiling the lacquer. An attempted correction was to lengthen the extensions and route them out below the body, but this didn't entirely solve the problem. (The condition persisted until the new 1956 design, when Corvette chief engineer Zora Arkus-Duntov relocated the exhaust tips to the rear fender extremities.)

After about the first 300 1954s,

Above: Styling was unchanged for 1954. Sales were disappointingly low. Above right: Optional 3-speed manual

transmission arrived late in the '55 season. Right: Most '55 'Vettes had the new 265 V-8. Large V in side script was the tipoff.

the two-handle hood release was replaced by a single-handle unit. At the 1900 mark, the three bullet-style air cleaners were dropped in favor of a two-pot type, used through the balance of the model run. A new cam also appeared in later engines, increasing horsepower to 155, but this was not revealed officially until 1955.

Early Corvettes had a few awkward features. To operate the choke, for example, you had to reach across or through the steering wheel with the left hand while operating the ignition with the right because both items were on the right. Subsequently the choke was moved to the left of the steering column, changing positions with the wiper control. Moisture in the rear license plate compartment caused the plastic lens to fog up, so Chevrolet thoughtfully inserted a container with two fabric bags full of a desiccant material to keep the lens clear.

Sales for 1954 proved disappointing. Even though the Corvette was now available in reasonable quantities from dealers, public response was mixed. Some analysts thought prospective buyers might have viewed it as neither fish nor fowl — not a true "road and track" machine, but not a genuine tourer, either. Purists objected to the

automatic transmission and the non-traditional styling. Sporting pleasure drivers didn't like the rude side curtains and manual folding top, and preferred fresh air heaters to the recirculating unit. There were some service problems, too, water leaks in particular. Actually, though, real mechanical problems were few. Service bulletins instructed dealers on fixing water leaks, synchronizing the three carburetors, and adjusting for smooth idle — hardly problems of major proportions. The engine, transmission, and driveline were all more than adequate, and reliable. But sales fell and inventories increased. Production slowed, then ground to a halt. At the close of 1954, up to 1500 cars remained

unsold. That's amazing in light of the popularity the 'Vette would later achieve.

Harley Earl had proposed a mild facelift for 1955 involving a new, wider eggcrate grille similar to that of the '55 Chevrolet passenger models. Budget limitations prevented this, however, so Corvette remained much as it had been before — with one big exception. This was the new 265-cid V-8 engine. It was ostensibly an option, but actually no more than 10 six-cylinder Corvettes were built for the entire model year. Here at last was the real get-up-and-go Chevrolet's sports car needed.

This new V-8 was sensational, producing a rousing 195

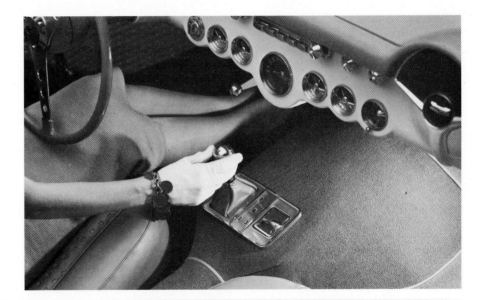

horsepower at 5000 rpm. It used the conventional passenger car block (3.75×3.00 bore and stroke), and actually weighed about 30 pounds less than the six. The performance gain was fantastic. It reduced the 0-60 time to between 8.5 and 9.0 seconds, and raised top speed proportionately, making the Corvette substantially faster than most V-8 sedans of the day. But perhaps more important, the V-8 Corvette was quicker than Ford's Thunderbird. Chevrolet took satisfaction in that.

Shortly after the start of 1955 production, the Pennant Blue color option was replaced by Harvest Gold, with contrasting green trim and dark green top, a popular combination. Metallic Corvette Copper was also made available, while Gypsy Red replaced the previous Sportsman Red. The latter came with white vinyl interior and red saddle stitching, tan carpet and top. Aside from color changes, the only exterior modification was a gold "V," overlaid on the letter "V" in the "Chevrolet" side script, to identify the V-8 models.

The 1955 bodies were smoother and slightly thinner in section than before, and workmanship was better. Early production cars

display holes in the frame rails for mounting the six-cylinder engine. The underside of the hood X-brace was replaced with a lateral brace, to clear the V-8's air cleaner. The V-8s also carried an automatic choke for the first time in production. Also, because the new engine revved higher than the six, the tachometer was changed to a 6000-rpm scale with 500-rpm increments. The electrical system became 12-volt, as on most '55 GM cars, although the six-cylinder engine was curiously listed with the 6-volt system. V-8s also featured an electric, rather than vacuum-operated, wiper motor, and foot-operated windshield washers were reinstated.

The transmission coupled to the V-8 was similar to the previous Powerglide, except that its vacuum

modulator was eliminated in keeping with all 1955 Chevrolet production. Kickdown was now governed solely by speed and throttle position. The big news, however, came late in the model run, when a small number of cars were built with a new close-ratio three-speed manual gearbox. The shifter was a small chrome stick, rising from the side of the tunnel and topped by a plain white ball. The boot around the lever was sealed to the floor with a bright metal plate showing the shift pattern. The rear axle ratio was shortened from the usual 3.55:1 Powerglide gearing to 3.70:1.

Unfortunately, 1955 proved to be another sales disappointment. Production totalled only 700 units for the model year. By the end of the Motorama-style cars, quality

and performance had been improved considerably, and the option list had been broadened. But the market was still elusive. Ford, meanwhile, was selling 16,155 Thunderbirds — roughly 23 times Corvette volume. Again, the Corvette's friends and foes alike asked: where do we go from here? One of the men who helped answer that question was Zora Arkus-Duntov.

Corvette had come very close to extinction in 1954, because of GM management's reservations about the car's sales potential. The attempt had been made, the car had been built; why not let the Corvette rest in the history books? The reason: Thunderbird. Ford's two-seater arrived at the height of the perennial battle between the industry's two leading companies.

For 18 months after mid-1953, Ford had engaged in production warfare, and swamped its dealers with more cars than they could ordinarily sell. Ford was determined to become number one—even if it almost had to give cars away. GM naturally responded in kind, and the production blitz was on. Both corporations took to the media. Each claimed victory, made counterclaims, and then accused the other of fudging the statistics. Nobody really knew who came out on top for 1955, but the competition was enough to change GM's attitude toward the Corvette. The two-seater field would not be left to the Thunderbird, which Corvette advertising soon referred to as a "scaled-down convertible."

The 1956 Corvette was among the last GM production cars designed in Detroit, before the design department was moved to the new Technical Center in Warren, Michigan. In a styling sense, the roots of the second-generation design were in three 1955 Motorama show cars, the Biscayne and two exercises dubbed LaSalle II. The Biscayne was a compact four-door hardtop painted light green, with a color-keyed interior. Appearance features included headlamps mounted inboard, parking lights placed in the fenders, and a grille made up of a series of vertical bars. Air scoops were positioned under the windshield on the cowl, and the passenger compartment floor was level with the bottom of the frame. The LaSalle II name appeared on a hardtop sedan and a roadster. Also carefully color-keyed, both had prominent vertical bar grilles, and displayed a styling feature the '56 Corvette would inherit: a concave section on the bodysides. This swept back from the front wheel wells, imitating the "LeBaron sweep" of the classic period. The greenhouse used for the liftoff hardtop that would be a new option for '56 was inspired mainly by a '54 show Corvette.

Opposite page, top: Biscayne show car previewed '56 model's toothy grille and bodyside sculpture. Opposite bottom: Sleek lines and V-8 muscle marked Corvette's maturity as a true sports car for 1956. This page, above and below left: Concave "cove" was often two-toned to enhance the new dashing appearance. Above: Lift-off hardtop gave all-weather protection, but installation usually called for two.

The '56 Corvette was all-new, and beautifully done—not overdone. It curved in all the right places, with contours that looked smooth and purposeful. Many aficionados believe that it and the lookalike '57 were the most beautiful Corvettes of the pre-1963 period. Exterior colors offered were Onyx Black, Venetian Red, Cascade Green, Aztec Copper, Shoreline Beige, Silver, and Polo White.

Besides its attractive styling, the '56 offered several improvements in passenger comfort, probably in response to the sales drubbing Chevy's car had taken from the less sporty but more luxurious Thunderbird. Among these were roll-up door windows and the optional hardtop, which provided sedan-like weather protection and better visibility.

The 265-cid V-8 was again borrowed from the passenger car line, the six now permanently banished from the sports car. Like the hottest standard Chevy mill, the

Corvette's V-8 had a four-barrel carburetor and 9.25:1 compression ratio, but used a special high-lift cam developed by Duntov that raised horsepower to 225 at 5200 rpm, and helped produce 270 foot-pounds of torque at 3600 rpm. The standard three-speed transmission and clutch were redesigned to handle the extra muscle. A 3.55:1 rear axle ratio was specified, but 3.27:1 gearing was optional. Powerglide automatic with the 3.55:1 cog was listed for $189 extra.

All this gave the '56 Corvette performance that belied its civilized looks. With manual gearbox and standard axle ratio, the car would turn 0-60 mph in 7.5 seconds and run the standing-start quarter mile in 16 seconds at 90-plus mph. It was capable of close to 120 mph right off the showroom floor. There was still some question about handling and stopping, however. Brakes— cast iron drums with 158 square inches of lining area—were a

weak point. They "faded into oblivion," as one tester said, after a hard application. Handling was good, but understeer was ever-present. The steering, however, was quick—just 3½ turns lock-to-lock. Weight distribution, at 52/48, was nearly perfect for a sports machine. In all, road behavior was greatly improved.

On the surface, the 1957 Corvette looked like the '56, but sported several significant under-the-skin changes. There was a larger V-8 option, a new four-speed gearbox introduced at mid-year, and (as Chevy boasted) up to one hp per cubic inch from the new "Ramjet" fuel injection system.

Although developed by Rochester Carburetor, Ramjet was strictly a GM design. It incorporated a special aluminum manifold, a fuel meter, and an air meter. Gulping in atmosphere, the air meter directed the air to the various intake ports, where a precise amount of fuel was

squirted in from a high-pressure pump driven off the distributor. Injection was available only for the new 283-cid enlargement of the 265, and gave it a rousing 283 bhp at 6200 rpm — the first time a mass-production engine developed one horsepower for each cubic inch of displacement. But the system had its bugs. Racing setups had to drop the fuel cutoff during acceleration to escape a flat spot; fuel nozzles absorbed heat and caused rough idling, or suffered from dirt deposits. Street users found the system hard to service. Only 240 of the 6339 Corvettes built for 1957 were equipped with Ramjet. When feeling good, though, it provided staggering performance: 0-60 mph in about 6.5 seconds, for example.

The 283 was produced by boring the 265 block about ⅛-inch to 3.875 inches. It also had higher compression and a higher-lift cam. Buyers had a choice of single (220 bhp) or dual (245 and 270 bhp) four-barrel carb setups plus two "fuelies" with 250 and 283 bhp. There was also a racing version nominally rated at 283 bhp. Valve lifters were hydraulic, except with injection. The 283 featured longer-reach spark plugs, carburetor fuel filters, larger ports, wider bearings, and oil-control piston rings. Dual exhausts on fuelies were connected by a crossover pipe, which equalized flow through each muffler, thus preventing uneven distribution and retarding rust.

A big step forward in Corvette performance was the May 1957 addition of a four-speed gearbox as a $188 option. It was essentially a three-speed Borg-Warner unit, with reverse moved into the tailshaft housing to make room for a fourth forward speed. The ratios were close at 2.20:1, 1.66:1, 1.31:1, and 1.00:1. Coupled to a fuelie engine and the optional 4.11 rear axle, it made the Corvette nothing less than a stormer. Tests showed 0-60 in 5.7 seconds, 0-100 in 16.8 seconds, the standing quarter mile in 14.3 seconds at 96 mph, and a top speed of 132 mph.

The experts still complained about handling and braking deficiencies, which Chevrolet solved with RPO 684, a comprehensive suspension package. It included front anti-sway bar and heavier springs; heavier rear leaf springs; larger, firmer shocks; ceramic-metallic brake linings with finned, ventilated drums; Positraction limited-slip differential; and a quick-steering adapter that reduced turns lock-to-lock from 3.7 to 2.9. Axle ratio options included 3.70:1, 4.11:1, and a root-pulling 4.56:1. With all this, you could order a car ready to race right out of the box — and race it did. Two production models finished 12th and 15th at Sebring 1957, the first GT-class cars across the line. The 12th place car ended up 20 laps ahead of the nearest Mercedes-Benz 300SL.

Undoubtedly, 1957 marked the Corvette's arrival as a sports car respected as much by the cognoscenti as the kids on the street. One European writer said: "Before Sebring, where we actually saw it for ourselves, the Corvette was regarded as a plastic toy. After Sebring, even the most biased were forced to admit that the Americans had one of the world's finest sports cars — as capable on the track as it was on the road. Those who drove and understood the Corvette could not help but reach that conclusion."

There was now no question about Corvette's survival. Model year production had risen from 3467 for 1956 to 6339 for '57. Thunderbird's exit from the two-seater market for 1958 (which Chevrolet foresaw well in advance) brightened hopes that production would exceed 10,000. Despite a dreadful 12 months for the industry in general, that goal was nearly reached. The exact count was 9168.

But while Corvette's place in the division lineup was now more or less assured, new approaches were in the works that would lead to a different kind of sports Chevy. For the car to continue, Chevrolet knew it would have to make money, yet Corvette had not yet recorded a profit. Additional sales volume and customer appeal became the orders of the day. In early 1957, General Motors had joined in the Automobile Manufacturers Association (AMA) resolution against any industry support for racing. All corporate competition efforts and publicity abruptly ceased. This policy, prompted by the National Safety Council and other groups, was based on the belief that racing activities and race-oriented automobile advertising inspired highway recklessness. The automakers officially withdrew from the sport for the next few

years. And in one way or another, this change in attitude was usually reflected in their products.

The 1958 Corvette was typical of the new corporate stance. Styling was busier, and weight was up. It didn't look—and wasn't—as lithe and agile as the 1956-57 models. Appearance changes were in keeping with then-current trends. The front sprouted four headlamps, with a chrome strip trailing back from each pair along the top of the fenders. Simulated louvers appeared on the hood, and chrome blossomed on the flanks, rear fenders, and trunklid. Overall length grew by nearly 10 inches, width by three inches. At 3000 pounds, the '58 weighed 100 pounds more than the '57.

Yet there were some useful changes. At Duntov's behest, instruments were regrouped in a pod for better legibility. A large grab bar was added for the passenger, and seatbelts were made standard. The fuel injection system was reworked for greater reliability, boosting output to 250 or 290 bhp at 6200 rpm. The carbureted 283s ranged from 230 to 270 bhp. The heavy-duty suspension option was retained.

Styling stayed mostly the same for '59. However, the fake hood louvers were erased, and Duntov saw to further detail refinements: inside door knobs were moved forward to avoid snagging clothes, the shift lever received a lockout T-handle, and the clutch was given a wider range of adjustment. The RPO 684 suspension got even harder spring settings. Still working on the brake problem, Chevy issued RPO 686—sintered metallic linings—which cost only $27 and were well worth it. Radius rods were fitted to reduce rear axle tramp.

The 1960 Corvette might have been a completely new car—the stillborn "Q" model, with all-independent suspension and a rear-mounted transaxle on a 94-inch wheelbase. The Q-model's styling directly prefigured that of the 1963 Sting Ray. But difficult times precluded production, so the '60 was mostly a carryover of the '59. However, more extensive use was made of aluminum—in clutch housings and some radiators, and the cylinder heads of fuel-injected engines. The aluminum heads were fine in theory, but suffered failures from internal flaws and tended to warp if the engine overheated. They were quickly dropped. Duntov replaced the stiff spring setup with double sway bars (the first rear suspension sway bar on an American car), which improved ride and handling. There were minor changes to the interior.

Corvette reached an international pinnacle at the 1960 Le Mans 24-hour race. Three cars entered by Briggs Cunningham in the big-engine GT class were excellent performers. One achieved 151 mph on the Mulsanne Straight, and the Bob

Above left: The Sebring SS special is shown with a bubble canopy intended, but never actually used, for long-distance events. That's Zora Arkus-Duntov behind the wheel. Center and bottom left: 1958 facelift brought a bulkier, chromier Corvette. Right: Redesigned 1958 cockpit grouped gauges and controls more conveniently. Copilot's grab bar was new, seatbelts made standard. Above and below: The '59 lost the washboard hood and decklid chrome strips.

replacing them with a mesh screen. Headlamp rims were painted in body color, also for a cleaner look.

Prices, meanwhile, had been climbing upward. The Corvette had listed (NADA base price) for $3149 in 1956, $3631 in 1958, and $3872 in 1960. For 1961 it was up to $3934; it would be $4038 for the '62. A fuel-injected car could run well over $5000 — some $1500 above what you would have paid for a '53. For this kind of money, buyers expected a lot of standard equipment. Chevrolet obliged in 1961 by including an aluminum radiator, parking brake warning light, dual sun visors, interior lights, and windshield washers.

Engine options for '61 were a rerun of the 1960 chart. The four-speed manual gearbox received an aluminum case, and a wider choice of gear ratios was offered for the three-speed unit.

Grossman/John Fitch car finished a respectable eighth. If Sebring '57 hadn't sufficiently impressed the Europeans, Le Mans '60 did.

The 1958-61 period saw the last of the small-block Corvette V-8s, and no less than seven variations were offered (see accompanying chart).

Styling for 1961-62 was a mild facelift of 1958-60, but highly effective. By that time, Bill Mitchell had relieved Harley Earl as chief of GM Design, and had created the racing Stingray, followed by the XP-700 show car. Both featured a new "ducktail" rear end; the show car's was used with front and

midsection roughly similar to that of the production 1958-60. The new tail received favorable reaction, and appeared for '61. To help make the car still fresher, Mitchell did away with the teeth that had marked Corvette grilles since 1953,

Corvette Small Blocks, 1958-61			
Years	bhp/rpm	induction	CR
1958-61	230/4800	1 4bbl	9.5
1958-61	245/5000	1 4bbl	9.5
1958-59	250/5000	fuel inj.	9.5
1958-61	270/6000	2 4bbl	9.5
1958-59	290/6200	fuel inj.	10.5
1960-61	275/5200	fuel inj.	11.0
1960-61	315/6200	fuel inj.	11.0

performance. The '62s featured a new 327-cid V-8 created by boring and stroking the 283 (4.00×3.25 inch), and the optional fuel injection was modified to suit. A 3.08:1 rear axle ratio was added for quiet cruising (available for the two lowest-horsepower engines only). The fine new powerplant formed the basis for Corvette muscle through 1965. For 1962 (and '63), it was available in four forms: 250 to 340 bhp with carburetion and 360 bhp with fuel injection. Improved torque gave the '62s better midrange performance, especially in the standing-start quarter mile. Typically, a 327 with the 3.70 differential would run it in 15 seconds at over 100 mph.

With the 1962 models, Corvette reached its peak of development. Thanks to Duntov, the car had long since shed whatever remained of its pedestrian origins. It was faster than ever, a superb handler, and functionally styled. With its new sintered-metallic brake linings, it could stop as well as it could go. It was also quite comfortable.

Corvette had received many important changes during its first 10 years, but none significantly altered the basic design. The X-braced frame and fiberglass body panels remained unaltered except in detail from 1953 through 1962. All that changed with the 1963 Sting Ray. It was a revolution—and a revelation. In addition to the roadster body type was a beautiful new grand touring fastback coupe. Both sold over 10,000 copies apiece, putting production for the model year over 21,500—

Over 85 percent of Corvette buyers were now ordering manual transmission, with a two-to-one preference for the four-speed.

The hairy 315-bhp injected engine was truly impressive when coupled to stump-pulling rear axle ratios. With the 4.11:1 axle, a big-inch 'Vette could clock 0 to 60 in 5.5 seconds and run the quarter mile in 14.2 seconds at 99 mph. Despite the ultra-short gearing, the car could do almost 130 mph.

For 1962, Mitchell completed his styling refinements. He deemphasized the concave bodyside "cove" by eliminating its chrome outline, and replaced the little teeth inside the reverse fender scoops with a grid. The mesh-type grille was blacked out, and a decorative strip of anodized aluminum was added to the rocker panels. The stiff springs were reinstated as an option; with their help, Dr. Dick Thompson won the SCCA A-production championship that year.

Semon E. "Bunkie" Knudsen replaced upward-bound Ed Cole as Chevrolet general manager, and began to push for higher production. The result: 14,531 cars were built for 1962, as opposed to the 10,939 the preceding year. Corvette had turned the profit corner in 1958. Now it was making an adequate return on investment as well.

It was also returning even better

Bill Mitchell's racing Stingray in show car trim, complete with Corvette badges.

about 50 percent better than any previous year. As the first of an entirely new line, the '63 has since received the recognition it deserves as a landmark design.

The engineering brief for 1963, according to Duntov, was "better driver and passenger accommodation, better luggage space, better ride, better handling, and higher performance." Styling Staff's contribution to these goals began in late 1959 with project XP-720 based on Mitchell's Stingray

racer (spelled as one word there and on production models after 1968). This closed coupe had a smooth fastback fuselage for which Mitchell had conceived an unusual split rear window. He'd had a rough time selling the idea to the practical Duntov. It made production, but only for 1963. As far as Mitchell was concerned, the later models with the one-piece backlight lacked a certain character. "If you take that off," he said, "you might as well

forget the whole thing."

The rest of the '63 package was practical as well as aggressively handsome. Among its novel styling features were hidden headlights mounted on pivoting sections that fit flush with and matched the front-end contour, a dipped beltline, and doors cut into the coupe's roof. A twin-cockpit dashboard, which had been present in one form or another since the 1953 Corvette, was retained. "It was a very fresh

Opposite page: 1963's new Sting Ray coupe (upper right) was subjected to extensive wind tunnel tests (center left). Potent "fuelie" V-8 (upper left) was up to 360 horses. Optional hardtop was still available for roadster (bottom). This page: Stunning coupe (top) nearly outsold the more popular roadster (left) in '63. New twin-cowl dash (above) worked quite well.

approach to two-passenger styling, and I think it worked remarkably well," said one GM designer.

Besides the coupe and roadster, other body styles had been contemplated, including a four-passenger version favored by Ed Cole. Both Mitchell and Duntov opposed it, saying the Corvette's distinction and personality would be compromised. A two-plus-two coupe (a style later introduced without visual success by sometime

rival Jaguar for the E-Type) made it as far as a full-size mockup before it, too, was nixed.

The production-ready '63 coupe and roadster were subjected to intensive wind tunnel evaluations at Cal Tech, and body engineers spent a great deal of effort on the inner structure. Compared to the '62 Corvette, the Sting Ray had nearly twice as much steel support built into its central body structure. But this was balanced by a reduction in fiberglass content, so

the finished product actually weighed a bit less than a '62. Wheelbase was shortened from 102 to 98 inches, the rear track was made two inches narrower, and frontal area was reduced by a square foot. Yet interior space was as good as before, and, thanks to the added steel reinforcement, the cockpit was stronger and safer. Other body features included curved door glass, cowl-top ventilation, increased luggage space, and an improved fresh air heater. Neither coupe nor roadster had an external trunklid as on the '62. This meant pulling the seatbacks down for access to the luggage space. The spare tire resided in an external hinged compartment that dropped down

21

to ground level for access.

Engines were carried over from 1962, but the brand-new body was matched by a modified chassis. Most of the changes were made at the back. For the first time, Corvette got independent rear suspension—a three-link type, with double-jointed open driveshafts on each side, plus control arms and trailing radius rods. A single transverse leaf spring (there was no room for coils) was mounted to the frame with rubber-cushioned struts, and the differential was bolted to the rear crossmember. The frame itself was a well-reinforced box shape. Front/rear weight distribution was improved to 48/52 from the previous 53/47. As a result of all this, ride and handling were much better, and axle tramp was virtually eliminated. A new recirculating-ball steering gear and three-link ball joint front suspension gave fewer turns lock-to-lock than before. Front brake drums were wider, and the brake system was now self-adjusting. Evolution dictated an alternator instead of a generator, positive crankcase ventilation, a smaller flywheel, and a new aluminum clutch housing.

Competition options for the Sting Ray were extensive, and designed mainly with the new coupe in mind. This hinted at GM's intent that it become a GT-class and SCCA contender. The heavy-duty hardware included uprated springs and shocks, stiffer anti-sway bar, metallic brake linings, optional Al-Fin aluminum brake drums, cast aluminum knock-off wheels, dual master brake cylinder, and a 36.5-gallon fuel tank. Full leather upholstery became a new interior option—for the sales competition.

Road testers raved about the exotic-looking new Sting Ray, with special comments reserved for the improved traction. The new car neither hopped during hard acceleration nor oversteered on tight bends. In driving the coupe through hard S-turns, *Road & Track* magazine reported: "Every time through we discovered we could have gone a little faster. We never did find the limit."

The excitement generated by the Sting Ray during its brief production life stemmed partly from its steady improvement each year. Contrary to the old Detroit axiom that you must add more trim and decoration on each succeeding model, Chevy actually removed the stuff. For 1964, the controversial split rear window disappeared, much to Mitchell's chagrin. Though it added "character," it also hindered rear vision. Also deleted were the fake hood louvers. Slotted wheel discs were added, and the '63's dummy roof vents were made functional to serve as interior air extractors. For 1965, the hood panel was planed smooth, and the front fender slots were opened up to duct heat out of the engine compartment. The roof extractor vents proved relatively inefficient so they were erased for 1966, when an eggcrate grille was adopted. For 1967, its fifth and final year, the Sting Ray reached near design perfection. The only changes this time were a single oblong backup light, revised

Far left, top and bottom: Ed Cole wanted a four-seat Sting Ray, perhaps to expand the Corvette's market. Result was this somewhat ungainly stretched-coupe mockup, which is as far as the idea went. Center, below: Four-place Sting Ray would have been an interesting GT alternative to Ford's Thunderbird, as this 1962 GM studio comparison photo suggests. Left: Coupe got a one-piece backlight for '64. Below: '64 ragtop was similarly cleaned up.

in competition. Duntov teamed with Jim Premo, who had replaced Harry Barr as Chevrolet chief engineer, to work the adaptation.

The first Mark IV displaced 396 cubic inches (4.09×3.75), mainly because GM policy in those days restricted cars of intermediate size and smaller to engines of less than 400 cid. Replacing the 365-bhp small-block option, it packed 425 bhp at 6400 rpm and 415 ft-lbs of torque at 4000 rpm thanks to 11:1 compression, solid lifters, and four-barrel carburetor. To handle this brute force, engineers added stiffer front springs, thicker front anti-sway bar, a new rear bar, heavier clutch, and a larger radiator and fan. Though the Mark IV engine weighed over 650 pounds, it did not adversely affect weight distribution, which remained near neutral at 51/49 front/rear. An aggressive-looking hood bulge and optional side-mounted exhaust pipes completed an impressive machine.

For 1966, a bore increase to 4.25 inches gave 427 cubes—and truly stupendous acceleration. With a car pulling the short 4.11:1 gearset, *Sports Car Graphic* magazine managed 0-60 mph in a nearly unbelievable 4.8 seconds, 0-100 in 11.2 seconds, and a maximum of 140 mph. The only car that could keep up with this Corvette was the 427 Cobra—and that was far less refined, with few of the Sting Ray's high-speed comfort features. Though the Cobra was a formidable competitor on the track, the big-inch Mark IV Corvette was really in a class by itself everywhere else.

Other engine happenings during the 1963-67 period bear mentioning. Fuel injection was dropped after 1965, mainly due to

front fender louvers, bolt-on instead of knock-off aluminum wheels, and an optional black vinyl covering for the roadster's removable hardtop.

Mechanically, each of the Sting Ray years brought important advancements. For 1964, the fuel-injected 375-bhp small-block engine developed 1.15 bhp per cubic inch — enough for a 0-100 mph time of 15 seconds flat. For 1965, four-wheel disc brakes were offered optionally, something enthusiasts had long been

demanding, and made for awesome braking power. Also that year came another big boost to performance: the Mark IV V-8.

Big-engined Corvettes were nothing new, of course. Mickey Thompson's specials for Daytona and other races had been seen with the 409 engine as early as 1962. Zora Arkus-Duntov had at first resisted the idea of a big-block option, but by '64 the need was apparent. Cars like the Shelby Cobra were not outselling Corvette, but they were trouncing it

23

Corvette Engines, 1963-67		
Years	**cid/induction**	**bhp/rpm**
1963-65	327/carb	250/4400
1963-67	327/carb	300/5000
1963	327/carb	340/6000
1965-67	327/carb	350/5800
1963	327/FI	360/6000
1964-65	327/FI	375/6200
1965	396/carb	425/6400
1966-67	427/carb	390/5400
1964-65	327/carb	365/6200
1966-67	327/carb	350/5800
1966	427/carb	425/6400
1967	427/carb	400/5400
1967	427/carb	435/5800

Corvette Model Year Production, 1963-67			
Year	**Coupe**	**Conv.**	**Total**
1963	10,594	10,919	21,513
1964	8,304	13,925	22,229
1965	8,186	15,376	23,562
1966	9,958	17,762	27,720
1967	8,504	14,436	22,940

high production costs, low sales, and the advent of the Mark IV program. Available engines by years are listed in the accompanying chart.

By the time Elliott M. "Pete" Estes had relieved Semon E. "Bunkie" Knudsen as Chevrolet general manager in 1965, the Corvette was permanently established in the divisional picture, with 20,000-plus sales a year. The production figures for each year of the Sting Ray indicate strong success.

The AMA's anti-performance resolution was ancient history in the mid-'60s, and Chevrolet set about preparing a competition reply to the big-block Cobra. Its answer was the Grand Sport, with a special 377-cid aluminum block V-8. Only five cars were built owing to GM's sudden cancellation of the project, which forced the GS to compete in SCCA class C-Modified. At Daytona 1963, all three Grand Sports ran 10 seconds a lap faster than the Cobras. Roger Penske won with one at Nassau the same year. Grand Sports were still racing as late as 1966, though by then they had been outclassed. The problem was not so much performance as numbers. Had Chevrolet been willing (and allowed by corporate higher-ups) to produce the minimum 100 cars necessary to qualify for a production class, the Grand Sport would have been unstoppable.

For 1966, Duntov showed his L-88 option for the 427 block—560 horsepower, the most powerful engine ever available for a Corvette. It sat in a chassis featuring the now-famous F-41 suspension package, heavy-duty

brakes, and Positraction. Unfortunately, the production Corvette just wasn't competitive with the 427 Cobra in SCCA's A-production class. The Cobra had almost as much horsepower, and was lighter by half a ton.

There *was* a place, however, for the big, strong, heavy Corvettes — endurance racing. In 1966, for example, Penske's team finished 12th overall and first in the GT class at the Daytona Continental. The next year, Dave Morgan and Don Yenko placed 10th overall and first in GT at Sebring. Bob Bondurant and Dick Guildstrand actually led the highly competitive GT class at Le Mans for several hours until their engine blew sky high. Endurance racing held great promise for the big-block Corvettes, but their potential wasn't exploited.

By this time, Chevrolet was committed to providing underground support to Can-Am racers like Jim Hall and Trans-Am Camaro teams like Penske's. In effect, Chevy had abandoned the sports car classes to Shelby's Cobras, and went to play on a different field where it had a better chance of winning. Given the restrictions of the GM bureaucracy, it was impossible for Chevy to work with an outside contractor the way Ford did with Carroll Shelby. It was equally impossible to turn a mass production car like the Corvette into an unqualified champion against hand-built machines created strictly for racing.

What was undeniable, though, was that the Sting Ray provided some of the most exciting motoring ever offered to Americans. It was fast, very capable on any kind of road, and wonderful to look at. Unfortunately, it was the shortest-lived Corvette design of all. Yet it sold nearly 120,000 copies, and remains among the most sought-after collector cars today. It brought Corvette development to a new peak of excellence and refinement.

Opposite page, above and below: Fuel injection made its final bow for 1965, the debut year of the big-block Mark IV V-8. Vertical fender vents and smoothed-off hood were new appearance refinements. This page: Coupe's roof vents were erased for '66 (top). All 427-equipped models got an aggressive-looking hood bulge (left). 1965's Mako Shark II show car (above) forecast the shape of 'Vettes to come.

The Sting Ray was hardly on the market a year when GM Styling Staff began planning its successor. This might actually have been a far different car than the one that emerged for 1968. Styling Staff had created a mid-engine design study, with a sharply raked front end, broad expanses of curved glass, skirted rear wheels, and nothing less than a functional periscope to serve as a rearview mirror. But over at Engineering Staff, the high cost of the necessary transaxle condemned the mid-engine configuration to the reject pile. Accordingly, the next series of production Vettes retained a very conventional mechanical layout, but bore a strong visual relationship to the experimental Mako Shark II show car of 1965.

The final styling work was directed by David Holls of the Chevrolet Studio, who couldn't have been a better choice. Holls had always been—and still is—an automobile connoisseur and an enthusiastic driver as well as a talented stylist. His personality was reflected in the finished product. Holls kept the ground-hugging snoot of the Mako II, but notched its fastback roofline slightly and added a Kamm-style rear deck with a spoiler. There was only one problem: air drag, which proved to be considerably greater than expected. Although the new design was scheduled to be introduced as a 1967 model, Duntov convinced division general manager "Pete" Estes to push it back to 1968 so wind tunnel tests could be made. These resulted in several changes: lower front fenders, a redesigned notchback, and—a surprise—a lower rear spoiler (the initial one had actually impeded air flow). Rear glass was also altered to improve visibility, and front fender louvers were

enlarged to improve engine cooling and reduce drag. An air dam was built into the front under-bumper pan, and pop-up headlights were hidden under panels that fit flush when closed.

The '68 Corvette retained the 1967 engine lineup, which meant you could order Duntov's mighty L-88 racing powerplant with up to 560 horsepower. It featured aluminum heads with 12.5:1 compression, oversize valves, aluminum intake manifold, and a small-diameter flywheel with beefed-up clutch. It was joined in 1969 by another racing mill, the aluminum-block ZL-1 dry-sump engine. This weighed 100 pounds less than the L-88, and listed for an astounding $3000 on the option book. These engines were not really street equipment, and very few were made.

At first, the '68 Corvette was not as well-liked as it came to be — probably because the 1963-67 design was such a hard act to follow. The new body was seven inches longer (most of it in front overhang), though wheelbase remained at 98 inches. Yet the interior was more cramped than the Sting Ray's, and there was less luggage space to boot. Some road testers bemoaned the new car's greater weight, up by 150 pounds compared to the '67. *Road & Track* summed up the case by saying the '68 was "highly reminiscent of certain older Ferraris, laid around a chassis that seemed fairly modern in 1962, but

Opposite page, top and center: The '67 was the last and best of the Sting Rays. Top 427 engine that year packed 435 bhp. Above and center left: Corvette lost its Sting Ray designation for 1968, though it still appeared on some press photos. Below: All-new, curvaceous '68 body concealed carryover chassis and drivetrains.

Top and center: Subtle refinements marked the '69 Corvette, including a revived "Stingray" nameplate. Opposite page, top and center: The 427 V-8 was stroked to 454 cid for 1970. Styling changes were minimal. Right: Cockpit (1970 shown) was criticized for being cramped. Far right: Top power for '71 was a 425-bhp 454.

is now quite dated by the march of progress. . . .We feel that the general direction of the change is away from Sports Car and toward Image-and-Gadget car." *Car and Driver*, on the other hand, called it "an almost irresistible temptation to buy American."

Subsequent developments indicated that somebody was listening at General Motors. Duntov, who had been temporarily shunted aside from Corvette

development, was restored to a position of considerable influence over the car's destiny. One change for 1969 was immediately evident: the "Stingray" designation (note the spelling), which had

disappeared for 1968, again adorned the flanks. Exterior door handles were cleaned up, black-painted grille bars replaced chrome, and backup lights merged with the inner taillights.

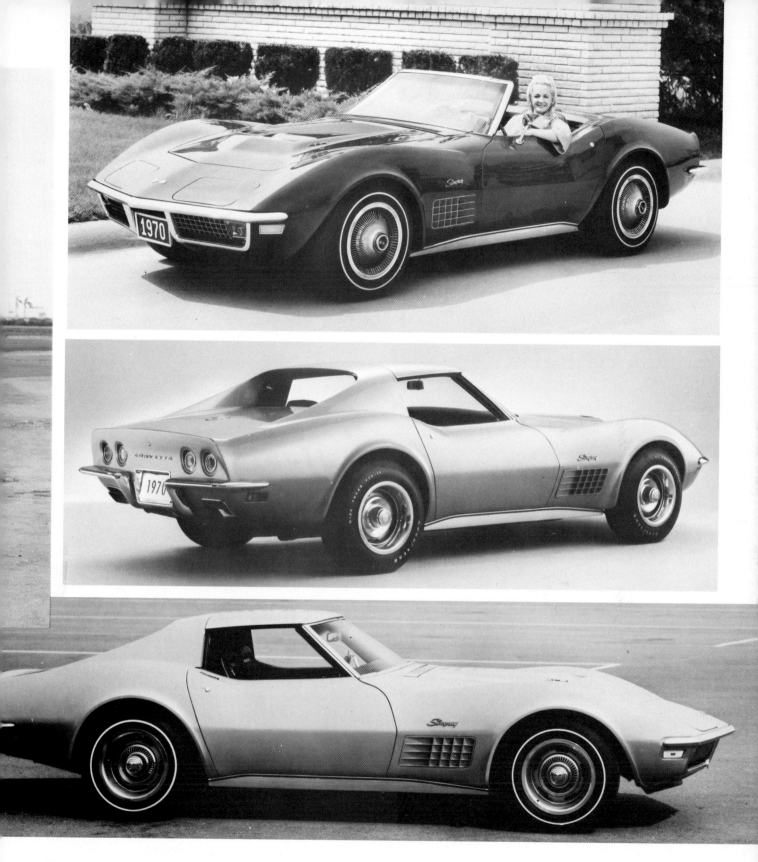

Handling was improved by wider-rim wheels, and a lot of shake was eliminated with a stiffer frame. The interior was reworked to create a bit more room for passengers and their odds and ends. The small-block engine was stroked to 350 cid (4.00×3.48), and offered either 300 or 350 bhp (one hp per cubic inch was nothing new by now). Four 427-cid engines were fielded, together with a vast array of axle ratios ranging from a super-low 4.56:1 to a long-striding 2.75:1. Still, the sports car crowd wasn't satisfied. Carped *Road & Track:* [It] lacks finesse; it's like using a five-pound axe when a rapier,

properly designed, could do as well." Yet *R&T*'s sister magazine, *Car Life*, was much more kind. While admitting these faults, plus a tendency "for things to fall off," *CL* insisted that "Corvettes are for driving, by drivers. . . . The Corvette driver will be tired of smiling long before he's tired of the car."

Interestingly, none of the controversy affected the money store. A production record had been set for '68 with 28,566 units. It was broken again with 38,762 for

model year 1969—a high that would stand until 1976. The formula was happily unchanged for the 1970 edition, although price zoomed to over $5000 base, up about $600 from the previous year. Sales were down substantially—to 17,316 units—but then 1970 was not the year 1969 had been throughout the industry. Coupes led convertibles in sales by five to three. The market adjusted in 1971 and '72, when production increased to 21,801 and

26,994, respectively.

The 427 block was enlarged to 454 cid for 1970, but this reflected increasingly tight federal emission controls and not a search for more go. This 4.25×4.00-inch unit actually developed less horsepower engine-for-engine than the 1968-69 427s. A still more powerful 465-hp version was planned, but was withdrawn due to certification problems. Meanwhile, the solid lifter small block, the LT-1, was producing a vigorous 370 bhp at 6000 rpm with 11:1 compression. Alas, this fine powerplant was also much tamed for '71, when compression sighed to 9.00:1, and output sank to a rated 330 bhp.

These were the last years for the high-compression, high-power Corvettes. The changes that occurred after 1970 are dramatic, as the accompanying chart demonstrates.

Thus, 1972 was a turning point— from high horsepower and high specific output to low emissions and low compression. There were no mechanical-lifter engines and no LT-1 for '73. The 350, producing

Corvette Engines, 1968-72			
Year	cid	bhp/rpm (SAE gross)	CR
1968	327	350/5800	11.0:1
1969-70	350	300/4800	10.25:1
1969-70	350	350/5600	11.0:1
1970	350	370/6000	11.0:1
1971-72	350	270/4800	8.5:1
1971-72	350	330/5600	9.0:1
1968-69	427	400/5400	10.25:1
1968-69	427	435/5800	11.0:1
1969	427	430/5200	12.5:1
1970	454	390/4800	10.25:1
1970	454	465/5200	12.25:1
1971	454	425/5600	9.0:1
1971-72	454	365/4800	8.5:1

Above left and right: Corvette stayed mostly the same again for 1972, but available horsepower was now on the decline, a sign of increasingly tighter emissions controls. Left: GM showed a couple versions of the Aero Coupe show car, mostly a mildly modified production '69. The later rendition shown here was dubbed "Sirocco." Note high-mount side mirrors and rooftop "periscope" blister. Below: Bowing to 5-mph bumper requirements, Chevy reworked the Corvette's nose for '73 with a body-colored, urethane grille surround. Also new that year was a domed hood with automatic air induction.

Above: The rear end followed the crash-bumper route for 1974. Although it looked nice, the change created more rear-end lift, to the detriment of high-speed stability. Right: The emphasis was more on luxury than performance in the mid-'70s, typified by this well-appointed 1974 interior. Below and bottom: The mostly unchanged '75 model made some wonder if the design hadn't been frozen. The 454 vanished this year, leaving just an emasculated 350 V-8 available.

270-330 bhp gross in 1972, was now rated at 190-250 bhp net. The only remaining Mark IV was a detuned 454 with 9.0:1 compression and 270 net horsepower, though even this was a performer in the context of 1973.

Physical and mechanical modifications in these years were minor. A burglar alarm became standard on '72s, ominous testimony to the rising rate of Corvette thefts. For 1973, the removable roof panels were eliminated (this year only) from the coupe, and the electrically operated wiper cover disappeared. A mandated change was the five mph crash bumper, made of polyurethane and painted body color, which considerably altered the car's frontal aspect.

The 'Vette appeared again mostly unchanged for 1974. A lot of people began to wonder if the design had been frozen. It had not, of course, but the marketing approach had changed along with the car's character. Corvettes were now much more expensive, appealing to a different clientele. The 350-cid open model with 250 net bhp started at $5500, and usually sold for $800-1000 more than that. It also weighed about 3500 pounds. It was a far cry from the light and nimble Sting Rays. Instead of hairy-chested performance, it was more oriented to comfortable touring. But production was up, and would continue rising in the years ahead.

The '74s did have some unobtrusive changes, mainly to meet federal regulations. The original Kamm-like tail was replaced with an energy absorbent rounded shape that was less effective at holding the rear end down. The consensus was that the loss in rear end adhesion didn't matter much given the decline in outright performance. (Tires, for example were changed from a 140-mph rating to 120-mph.) One bright spot was the optional "gymkhana" suspension using the tried-and-true formula of

Continued on page 49

Corvette's long-traditional crossed-flags emblem (above) has graced America's only true sports car since 1953.

Almost all 1955 Corvettes were fitted with the brilliant 265 V-8 engine. To mark its presence, Chevy exaggerated the "V" in the side script (inset). Metal cover hid the fabric top when stowed (right), one of Harley Earl's many styling innovations on the first-generation Corvette. Top goes up easily, but looks somewhat ungainly (far right). After some 30 years, the early Corvette still has loads of eye appeal (below). Grille "teeth" were typical of '50s styling. A mild facelift was planned for '55, but sagging sales at the time precluded it.

Corvette was totally restyled for 1956 (below), and now had the looks to match the performance of its smooth, high-winding V-8. Concave bodyside sculpturing, sometimes called the "cove," was a styling idea adapted from earlier GM Motorama show cars. Appearance was mostly unchanged for 1957 (right), but the big news was the optional 283-cid V-8 with fuel injection. Optional lift-off hardtop was another show car idea, and proved popular.

Appearance was bulked up for 1958, and the car stayed with this basic look through 1960 aside from minor trim changes. Top power for 1959 (above) was the 290-bhp fuel-injected 283.

Bill Mitchell's "ducktail" rear-end treatment for 1961 (below and right) was a successful update of Harley Earl's 1958 design, and previewed the forthcoming Sting Ray.

The 283 V-8 was bored out to 327 cubes for '62, when Mitchell cleaned up the 'Vette's lines even more, with a blacked-out grille and rocker panels.

Other '62 spotter's points are the absence of a chrome molding around the cove and a vertical grid in place of the teeth on the reverse front fender scoop.

The formidable Stingray racer (opposite top and inset) was campaigned with distinction in SCCA competition by Dr. Richard Thompson in 1959-60. Bill Mitchell built it using the chassis of the 1957 Sebring SS development "mule" for which he paid just one dollar.

After its racing career, the Stingray got official GM sanction, and toured the show circuit with the trim and emblems shown. The Mako Shark (inset and opposite bottom), built in 1961, was another forecast of the '63 Sting Ray. Its paint graduated from black to silver, simulating the colors of its namesake. Only five Corvette Grand Sports (below) were built before GM pulled the plug on Chevy's GT racing effort in 1963.

The production Corvette Sting Ray set the automotive world on its ear in 1963, with sensational new styling, muscular engines, and all-independent suspension. Besides the traditional roadster model (below), a stunning companion coupe (right) appeared with a unique divided backlight, a distinctive Bill Mitchell touch.

Although lighter than previous Corvettes, the Sting Ray was structurally more rigid and its styling aerodynamically more efficient. Available horsepower went up to 360 bhp from the "fuelie" 327 V-8, identified by tri-color front fender insignia. Today, the '63s are perhaps the most desirable Corvettes of all,

particularly the split-window coupes. Note the simulated air intakes (removed on later Sting Rays) on the roadster's hood. Handsome cast-aluminum wheels with knock-off centers were a desirable option then, and are a real find today. Bulging fender contours started the "coke-bottle" styling fad that swept Detroit in the late '60s.

CORVETTE
4-4-63
CHEVROLET

Sting Ray styling was progressively cleaned up and refined during the fourth generation's brief five model-year life, the shortest of any 'Vette series. The '63 split-window coupe (below) contrasts with its 1966 counterpart (above), which differs in its functional front fender louvers and absence of roof "gills" behind the doors. New that year was the 427-cid version of the

big-block Mark IV V-8. The roadster continued to out-number coupes from 1963 to '67, and was still available with an all-weather lift-off hardtop. The '66 model is shown (above) against the backdrop of Detroit's skyline.

Fuel injection put in its last appearance for 1965 on the 375-bhp 327. Sting Ray power reached its peak in 1967 with 435 bhp from the 427 with 11.0:1 compression. All Mark IVs got a beefed-up chassis and special hood bulge.

The beautiful Sting Ray was a tough act to follow, which may be why its 1968 successor received mixed reviews. The previous year's engine lineup was carried over, as was most of the chassis. The shape — an adroit mix of curves and planes — was clearly patterned after that of the Mako Shark II show car of 1965, refined by wind tunnel testing. The coupe featured a new tunneled backlight and twin panels that lifted off to reveal the industry's first T-bar roof design, another trend-setter.

The 1968 Corvette (above) was shorn of its Sting Ray designation, but that reappeared for 1969 (below and bottom) — spelled as one word. Changes included a beefed-up frame, cleaned-up exterior trim, and a new 350-cid V-8, essentially a stroked 327. Production was up by over 10,000 units. The top 427 engine was belting out 435 bhp for 1968 and '69 on its high 11.0:1 compression ratio. Special racing engines with up to 560 horses were listed, but weren't easy to get hold of.

Continued from page 32

higher-rate springs and firmer shocks. Luxury options proliferated: electric windows, vacuum assisted brakes, integrated air conditioning, stereo tape deck, and leather upholstery. Even with all this fluff, a 350-cid Corvette would still do 0-60 in 7.5 seconds and easily exceed 125 mph. It also returned about 14 mpg—by Corvette standards, an improvement in "economy."

The Mark IV engine vanished after 1974, and the 350-cid V-8 had to be progressively detuned to satisfy Washington:

Year	bhp/rpm	CR
1975	205/4800	9.0
1976	210/5200	9.0
1977	210/5200	9:0
1978	185/4000	8.9

That the Corvette remained a performance car at all despite the detuning in these years has often gone unnoticed. The 1977 version, for example, proved there was still lots of spunk left. *Road & Track* reported "the fastest time we've ever recorded through our slalom test—faster than the Porsche Turbo Carrera." It did the 0-60 sprint in 6.8 seconds, a half-second quicker than the 1973 test car.

By its silver anniversary year, 1978, Corvette was safely enshrined in the lexicon of American performance. It might now be heavy, emission-controlled, and safety-bumpered, but it remained one of the few interesting new American cars still around. It had also changed relatively little in character or size (it had gained only three inches in length since 1968), a tribute to the durability of the basic design and those who had directed the changes that were made to it.

Maintaining its reputation for style and stamina may be largely credited to Zora Arkus-Duntov. In 1977 he was asked to sum up his 25-year experience in one word. He chose "struggle." When interviewer John Lamm asked him "With whom?", Duntov smiled and said: "Whoever came to have an

Corvette sales were brisk in the '70s, Chevy saw no reason for big changes. This is the '76.

The tunnelback roof made its last appearance for 1977. 'Vette was still a quick sprinter.

Mulsanne show car of the late '60s predicted the 1973-74 "soft" nose and tail treatments.

opinion different than mine."

For the first time since 1968, there was something approaching a major appearance change for the '78 Corvette. This was a fastback rear window that wrapped around to the sides. It gave the car a completely different profile compared to the vertical window and "flying buttress" roof used up to that point, and nicely complemented the "soft" nose and tail adopted for 1973-74. Only problem was, the window looked like it should open hatchback fashion for better luggage access, but it didn't. Still, it was the feature that made the fourth generation's gradual styling metamorphosis complete.

To celebrate the Corvette's 25th birthday, Chevrolet issued not one, but two limited production "specials," both highly sought-after today. One, appropriately named the Silver Anniversary Model, featured two-tone paint (silver over a grey lower body with separating pinstripe) plus nice-looking alloy wheels carrying fat Goodyear GT raised white letter radial tires. The lift-off roof panels were made of tinted glass instead of steel, and the interior was color-keyed to the exterior.

The other '78 special was a facsimile of the Corvette pace car used for that year's Indianapolis 500. It was decked out with a black upper body and silver-metallic lower body, plus the alloy wheels and wide tires. It also carried

prominent front and rear spoilers, which some viewed as ruining the car's basic shape. A novel touch was the inclusion of a package of identifying "Pace Car" decals for the owner to apply if desired to complete the effect. Upholstery was your choice of silver leather or a silver leather/grey cloth combination. The seats used were a new design scheduled for all 1979 models.

With power windows, electric rear window defroster, air conditioning, sport mirrors, and other goodies, the Pace Car listed for more than $4000 above the base Corvette—a formidable $13,653. Despite that, demand for it was high—so much so that a few bogus ones appeared. At the time, the "real" Replicas fetched upwards of $28,000. This tempted some owners of standard 'Vettes to paint their cars to match, and then to try to pass them off as "factory" Pace Cars. The giveaway, of course, was the seats: only the true Pace Car replica has seats which are similar to, but not exactly the same as, the ones in production '79s. Naturally, all this created anguish for dealers—not to mention buyers looking for an instant collector's item. In fact, it still does. Chevrolet would remember this painful experience a few years later.

Chevy trotted out two factory specials to mark Corvette's 25th birthday. The Silver Anniversary model (far left and left) displays the car's new fastback roof. Note special decklid insignia. Indy Pace Car Replica (below left and right) came with the L-82 high-performance V-8. Owner applied the decals.

Corvettes of the Present

The 1980 Corvette, like its predecessors, owed much to the car's competition experience, which began in the late 1950s. It was in the crucible of all-out racing that many improvements were hammered out, and later adapted to production vehicles.

Today, of course, Corvette is one of the most coveted cars on the road. It is perhaps the only American car with an appeal so broad that its fans range from teenagers to septuagenarians. Its history spans more than a quarter century now, filled with memorable models like the split-window '63 coupe, the racing Grand Sport and SR-2, the "fuelies" of the '50s. Each year, it seems, brings a new Corvette that refuels enthusiasm for the car. In fact, about the only

thing that interests car buffs more than details about this year's Corvette is information on *next* year's Corvette.

That's been particularly true since 1968 and the start of the long-lived fifth generation design. As early as 1972, for example, some automotive journals were forecasting the "sixth generation" Corvette would be a mid-engine design. Later, it appeared an all-new model would debut for 1980 with styling based on the Aerovette show car. In fact, the Aerovette toured the show circuit in the early '70s so GM management could gauge public reaction to a mid-engine Corvette. Aerovette *was* a smash hit, but it was not readied for production. The reason: there was no need for it at

the time. the post-1967 Corvette was selling just fine, thank you. The public continued to buy Corvettes in record numbers during the '70s. Chevy was obviously doing something right despite leaving the car basically untouched for what some felt were too many years. *Road & Track* magazine had an answer. It began its test of the 1978 model by asking, "An All-American Sports Car? Yup, it really is, and as we've said before, it's a heck of a bargain." In 1979, the magazine's testers compared the Corvette favorably to any other sports car made, and gave it high marks, particularly its engine: "The Chevrolet V-8 is quiet, even at speeds up to 90 mph. It's still the fastest in a straight line and has gobs of torque, a very important

attribute for most American drivers. Mechanically simple, it's the sort of engine you can forget about and yet still rely on."

Recently, there has been a lot of talk about future Corvette engines, with perhaps the most interest centered on a turbocharged V-6. In the past couple of years, Chevrolet has built several "testing-the-waters" turbo cars, among them the Turbo Chevette

Rally and, in 1979, the Turbo Corvette. The latter is actually a "turbo/fuelie," featuring fuel injection as well as turbocharging. It was developed by Chevrolet's Product Promotion Engineering Department as a demonstration project, and was trotted around to several automotive journals for testing. The result was predictable: they all loved it.

The turbocharger is made by

Garrett AiResearch, one of the pioneers in this field. The injection system is specially modified for use with the turbo. The combination is interesting because of several refinements added by Chevrolet engineers. One of these is a special manifold pressure sensor, developed by Bendix, which informs an on-board computer on the amount of turbo boost provided. The computer then

Technical Highlights

Here's a brief year-by-year review of Corvette engineering and styling developments:

1953—Corvette introduced. Zora Arkus-Duntov joins GM.
1954—Work begins on optional V-8 engine.
1955—Duntov-prepared Corvette exceeds 150 mph at Daytona Beach.
1956—First major design change. Optional hardtop available.
1957—Factory fuel injection offered. Three "Positraction" axles available: 3.70:1, 4.11:1, and 4.56:1. Heavy-duty racing suspension offered. Five optional 283-cid engines added: 245 bhp (carbureted), 270 bhp (carbureted), 250 bhp (fuel-injected), 283 bhp (fuel-injected) and 283 bhp (race version, fuel-injected).

1958—Top engine option boosted to 290 bhp (fuel-injected)
1959—Metallic brake linings offered.
1960—First year for aluminum heads and aluminum radiators. Top engine option boosted to 315 bhp (fuel-injected).
1961—Aluminum radiator made standard. Direct-flow exhaust system offered as no-cost option.
1962—327-cid engine introduced producing 360 bhp in fuel-injected form.
1963—Second major design change with split-window coupe and "Sting Ray" designation. Sintered metallic brakes optional. Off-road exhaust system available. Power steering added. Pop-up headlights introduced. Option Z06, special performance package for coupes only, made available.
1964—One-piece rear window substituted on coupe. Top engine option boosted to 375 bhp (fuel-injected). Transistorized ignition added.

1965—Four-wheel disc brakes with four-piston calipers now standard equipment. M22 4-speed, close-ratio heavy-duty transmission added to option list. Telescopic steering column offered.
1966—Top engine option is carbureted "Turbo-Jet V-8," 427 cid and 425 bhp. Fuel injection discontinued.
1967—Top engine option is 435-bhp 427 with aluminum cylinder heads. Wheel width increased to 6 inches from 5½ inches.
1968—Third major design change. Sting Ray name dropped. Wheel width increased to 7 inches. Turbo-Hydra-matic transmission introduced.
1969—350-cid engine introduced. Stingray (one word) name revived. Wheel width increased to 8 inches. Steering column lock standardized. Steering wheel diameter reduced from 16 inches to 15 inches.
1970—Turbo-Jet 454-cid engine introduced. Top option is 390-bhp LS5. LS7 with 460 bhp made available to racers only.

adjusts fuel flow for smooth, powerful running. Another sensor signals the distributor to retard timing if pre-ignition (knocking) is about to occur. The turbo/fuelie system was designed around a modified lower-compression version of the L-48 engine and not the higher-compression L-82 powerplant. A Turbo Hydra-matic transmission is used instead of a four-speed manual gearbox,

apparently so the car would be easier for GM corporate types to test drive. Regardless, the car is fast. It'll hit 30 mph in about 2.2 seconds and 70 mph in 8.5 seconds. That's a tad faster than the stock '79 L-82 with four-speed that uses more gas. Many believe turbocharging is definitely part of the Corvette's future, and this development car may forecast just such a move.

A few Corvette owners have also

played with turbocharging. Former race driver Don Yenko built an absolute screamer in 1978, and Bob Larson built a twin-turbo car in 1979. Larson, who owns his own engineering company, took a

350-cid LT1 small-block introduced. 1970 production only 17,316.
1971—ZR1 factory racing option available with 330-bhp 350 engine. ZR2 option features 454-cid 425-bhp engine. 454-cid LS6 with 425 bhp introduced.
1972—Engine output now quoted in SAE net figures. Top engine option is 454-cid LS5 with 270 bhp. Anti-theft alarm system standardized.
1973—Energy-absorbing front bumper introduced. Coupe rear window fixed. LT1 engine discontinued. L82 engine with 270 bhp introduced. Top engine option is LS4, at 454 cid and 275 bhp.
1974—Last year for dual exhausts. Last year for 454-cid engines. Rear end restyled to accommodate 5-mph crash bumpers.
1975—Catalytic converters added. Last year for roadster; only 4629 built. Only engine option is L82, down to 205 bhp. High-energy ignition system introduced.
1976—L82 engine option now rated as 210

bhp. Aluminum wheels offered at $300 option.
1977—Leather seats standard. Wipe/wash and dimmer switches moved to steering column. Power steering, power brakes standard.
1978—Body styling altered to "fastback" roof. Limited-production Silver Anniversary, Indianapolis Pace Car models offered. Windshield wiper control moved back to dash. L82 engine uprated to 220 bhp.
1979—60-series radial tires offered as $226 option. L82 now rated at 225 bhp. New lightweight bucket seats introduced (first used on '78 Indy Pace Car).
1980—Front and rear spoilers integrated in redesign of long-running body style. Special 305-cid "California" engine introduced to meet emissions limits in that state only. Curb weight reduced 250 pounds to approximately 3230 pounds.
1981—New fiberglass reinforced plastic monoleaf rear spring adopted on models

with automatic transmissions. Thinner side glass, stainless steel exhaust manifolds, and lighter materials for engine and interior components help reduce weight. L-81 version of 350 V-8 gets magnesium rocker covers and auxiliary electric cooling fan. Quartz clock and 6-way power seats made standard.
1982—Drivetrain slated for 1983 introduced in otherwise unchanged model. L-83 powerplant features dual throttle-body fuel injection (TBI) system, which Chevrolet calls "Cross Fire Injection." Only transmission offered is four-speed overdrive automatic. In-tank electric fuel pump adopted. Special Collector Edition model features an opening rear hatch, a Corvette first.
1983—"New" restyled model debuts—10 inches shorter, 500-600 pounds lighter, and about as wide as previous models. Smoother bodywork, greater glass area, alloy wheels, and ultra-low profile tires are styling highlights.

stock 1976 engine with 780-cfm pressurized carburetor and added a pair of turbochargers. The result was an absolute rocket ship. There was also the racing twin-turbo Trans Am Corvette of Greg Pickett, which was used as a sort of testbed for possible production drivetrains. Racing has always served as a proving ground for newly designed components, particularly in the Corvette's case. Four-wheel disc brakes, the "rock crusher" manual transmission, and non-metal body pieces are just a few examples from the past. This kind of experimentation received considerable publicity from the enthusiast press and served to focus attention on what the next Corvette may — or may not — be.

The 1980 Corvette carried a hint of what was to come for 1981-82. It was lighter than the '79 by about 250 pounds, and significantly the weight-trimming effort was extended on the '81 and '82 models. Less weight means performance levels can be maintained while improving fuel

economy. It was obvious from the 1980 car that engineering efficiency would be a keynote in the next generation of Corvettes. Aerodynamics is another. The integral front and rear spoilers adopted for 1980 help reduce air drag, which also translates into increased fuel economy from a powerful V-8.

The 1981 Corvette was mostly a copy of the 1980 model, although there were some subtle changes. For example, the steel transverse monoleaf rear spring was replaced by one made of reinforced plastic for a saving of 33 pounds. Other weight-saving

engineering measures included use of thinner glass for the doors and roof panels and a stainless steel (instead of cast iron) exhaust manifold. Engine choices were reduced to a single 350-cid V-8 with four-barrel carburetor. Listed as the L-81, the engine carried new magnesium rocker covers and an auxiliary electric fan to supplement the regular engine-driven fan. In line with other 1981 GM cars, Corvette gained the firm's Computer Command Control electronic emissions control system. This provided more precise fuel metering, and also governed lockup of the automatic

Top: Turbo Vette 3 experimental was shown in 1981. Is it a forecast of a "blown" production model? Above and top right: A

fiberglass rear leaf spring and thinner glass pared more pounds for '81. Only one 350-cid V-8 was listed, and manual shift

put in its last appearance. Right: The '82 previewed the more fuel-efficient drivetrain to be used for '83.

transmission's torque converter clutch. The interior was spiffed up with power seats and a quartz clock as standard. The car rolled on 15×8-inch wheels shod with P225/70R-15 radial tires. Two tire options were available — P225/70R-15 raised white letter radials or super-low-profile P225/60R-15 RWL covers, all from Goodyear. That was it: a few cosmetic changes, some weight reduction, some refinements to engine, chassis and interior, but basically the same car as produced in 1980 and before.

The 1982 Corvette is essentially the same as the '81, with one important exception: its drivetrain is the one developed for the redesigned (some say "all new") 1983 Corvette. The engine is the familiar 350-cid V-8 but with a newly developed twin throttle-body fuel injection system, called Cross-Fire Injection, instead of a carburetor. The four-speed manual gearbox of previous years is gone, replaced by a four-speed overdrive automatic transmission. This features a lockup torque converter clutch effective on all forward gears except first. TBI was adopted for its more precise fuel metering compared to a carb, as well as for its beneficial effects on emissions levels. The Cross-Fire V-8, intriguingly dubbed L-83 in factory parlance, produces 200 bhp, 10 more than the L-81. There's also an in-tank electric fuel pump and a door in the hood that opens in response to the engine's demand for more air.

Chevy's experience with the bogus 1978 Pace Car Replicas figured into its decisions regarding the 1982 Collector Edition Corvette. This model, which more or less signals the last of the "big" 'Vettes, is being built only as needed to satisfy customer orders, not as a proportion of total production. To help prevent someone from turning a standard model into a Collector Edition, Chevy has also fitted special vehicle identification number plates. A more obvious feature on this limited-production special is its frameless lift-up hatch window, an item some critics said the Corvette should have had when the fastback roof was added for '78. Other standard touches include cloisonné emblems on hood, rear deck, and steering wheel; unique silver-beige metallic paint; graduated "shadow" contrasting paint stripes on hood and bodysides; bronze-tinted glass roof panels; and finned, cast-aluminum wheels styled like the ones offered as an option on the 1963 Sting Ray. Inside are special silver-beige cloth upholstery, leather door trim, leather-wrapped steering wheel, and luxury carpeting. Exclusivity

Above: Fuel injection with cross-ram manifold returned for the first time since 1965 to mark the last of the "big" 'Vettes. Far right: The 1982 Collector Edition shows off its frameless glass hatch, special paint, and bronze-tint roof panels.

never comes cheaply, but the Collector Edition's $19,000 list price isn't outrageous for the times.

Test reports on the '82 indicate the L-83 is silky smooth and quite powerful, though acceleration is a bit off compared to the '81 four-speed manual version. Handling is still somewhat clumsy, with a distinct lack of feel through the standard power steering and mushy cornering response. The optional "gymkhana" suspension is

still available to sharpen up the car's road manners—at a noticeable penalty in ride comfort.

GM officials as much as admitted that the '82 Corvette was yet another stopgap model. But, they promise it's the *last* one based on the fifth-generation design. The long-awaited all-new 'Vette is at last waiting in the wings.

Corvette in Competition

1955
- Stock Car Record Time, Pike's Peak Hill Climb

1956
- 150 mph at Daytona Beach (Zora Arkus-Duntov, Betty Skelton, John Fitch)
- 9th Overall, 12 Hours of Sebring (John Fitch, Walt Hangsen)
- 1st in Class B, Nassau (Ray Crawford)
- SCCA C-Production Champion (Dr. Richard Thompson)
- 1st in Class C, Pebble Beach Production Car Race

1957
- 1st in Class, 12 Hours of Sebring (John Fitch, Piero Taruffi)
- SCCA B-Production Champion (Dr. Richard Thompson)
- SCCA B Sports/Racing Champion (J. R. Rose)

1958
- 1st in GT Class, 12 Hours of Sebring (Jim Rathmann, Dick Doane)
- 1st in Sports Car Division, Pike's Peak Hill

Climb (Ak Miller)
- SCCA B-Production Champion (Jim Jeffords, "Purple People Eater" SR-2)
- Pacific Coast Road Racing Champion, B-Production (Andy Porterfield)

1959
- SCCA B-Production Champion (Jim Jeffords)

1960
- 1st in Class, 12 Hours of Sebring (Chuck Hall, Bill Fritts)
- 8th Overall, 24 Hours of LeMans (Bob Grossman, John Fitch)
- SCCA C Sports/Racing Champion (Dr. Richard Thompson, "Sting Ray Special")
- SCCA B-Production Champion (Bob Johnson)

1961
- 1st in GT Class, 12 Hours of Sebring (Delmo Johnson, Dale Morgan)
- 1st in Class, Pike's Peak Hill Climb (Ak Miller)
- SCCA B-Production Champion (Dr. Richard Thompson)

1962
- 1st in Class, Daytona Continental
- SCCA A-Production Champion (Dr. Richard Thompson)
- SCCA B-Production Champion (Don Yenko)

1963
- SCCA B-Production Champion (Don

Yenko)
- 1st in Prototype Class, Nassau (Roger Penske)

1964
- 1st in GT Class, Daytona Continental (Grand Sport) (Roger Penske, George Wintersteen, Dick Guldstrand, Ben Moore)
- SCCA B-Production Champion (Frank Dominianni)

1965
- SCCA Midwest Division Champion, A-Production (John Martin)
- SCCA Midwest Division Champion, B-Production (Brad Brooker)
- SCCA Southwest Division Champion, B-Production (Zoltan Petrany)

1966
- 1st in GT Class, Daytona Continental (Roger Penske, George Wintersteen, Dick Guldstrand, Ben Moore)
- 1st in GT Class, 12 Hours of Sebring (Penske, Wintersteen, Guldstrand, Moore)

1967
- 1st in GT Class, 12 Hours of Sebring (Don Yenko, Dave Morgan)
- Ran 1st in GT Class, 24 Hours of LeMans, until engine failed (Bob Bondurant, Dick Guldstrand)

1968
- 1st in Class, 12 Hours of Sebring (Dave Morgan, Hal Sharp)

1969
- SCCA Class A-Production Champion (Jerry Thompson)
- SCCA Class B-Production Champion (Allan Barker)

1970
- SCCA Class A-Production Champion (John Greenwood)
- SCCA Class B-Production Champion (Allan Barker)

1971
- 1st in GT Class and 4th Overall, 24 Hours of Daytona (Tony DeLorenzo, Don Yenko)
- 1st in GT Class, 12 Hours of Sebring (John Greenwood, Dick Smothers)
- SCCA A-Production Champion (John Greenwood)
- SCCA B-Production Champion (Allan Barker)

1972
- Ran 1st in Class, 24 Hours of LeMans, until part failed (John Greenwood)
- SCCA A-Production Champion (Jerry Hansen)
- SCCA B-Production Champion (Allan Barker)

1973
- 1st in Class, 12 Hours of Sebring (John Greenwood, Ron Grable)
- SCCA B-Production Champion (Bill Jobe)
- SCCA B-Stock Solo II Champion (John Anderson)
- SCCA B-Prepared Solo II Champion (Craig Johnson)

1974
- SCCA A-Production Champion (J. M. Robbins)
- SCCA B-Production Champion (Bill Jobe)
- SCCA B-Stock Solo II Champion (Steve Eberman)

1975
- 1st Overall, Trans Am Series (John Greenwood)
- SCCA A-Production Champion (Frank Fahey)

1976
- SCCA A-Production Champion (Gene Bothello)
- SCCA B-Production Champion (Howard Park)
- SCCA B-Stock Solo II Champion (Orin Butterick)

1977
- SCCA A-Production Champion (Steve Anderson)
- SCCA B-Production Champion (Bruce Kalin)
- SCCA B-Prepared Solo II Champion (Jack McDonald)

1978
- 1st Overall, Trans Am Category II (Greg Pickett)
- SCCA A-Production Champion (Elliott Forbes-Robinson)
- SCCA B-Production Champion (Andy Porterfield)
- SCCA B-Stock Solo II Champion (David M. Wright)
- SCCA B-Prepared Solo II Champion (John J. Seiler)
- SCCA B-Stock Ladies Solo II Champion (Sandra Schneider)

1979
- 1st, Vintage Car Races, Riverside, California (Bob Paterson, driving Grand Sport #003)
- 1st Overall, Trans Am Category I (Gene Bothello)
- SCCA B-Production Champion (Andy Porterfield)
- SCCA B-Stock Solo II Champion (Steve Eberman)
- SCCA B-Prepared Solo II Champion (Larry Park)
- SCCA B-Stock Ladies Solo II Champion (Janet Saxton)

1980
- SCCA B-Production Champion (Jerry Hansen)
- SCCA B-Prepared Solo II Champion (Gerald Kuhn)
- SCCA B-Prepared Ladies Solo II Champion (Chris Kuhn)

Corvettes of the Future

A great many changes—some subtle, some striking—mark the 1983 Corvette as "America's only true sports car" enters its 30th year of production. It is not the totally new mid-engine design that has been rumored since 1970—but it is very different from the 1968-82 generation and definitely a high-tech automobile.

It is not powered by a V-6, as some suspected it might be. Instead it carries a fuel-injected 350-cubic-inch V-8, which drives the rear wheels just like every Corvette since Job One. The standard transmission is an economy-oriented automatic with overdrive gearing and a lockup torque converter clutch activated by sophisticated engine electronics. The bottom line is mileage expected to be in the

22-25 MPG range on the highway. Brakes are four-wheel power-assisted discs that will stop turbine-style wheels of ultra-lightweight alloy manufactured by a California firm. Tires are squat, low-profile radials, which are much quieter than those used on the '82 models. The frame, body panels, and bumpers are lighter, too. The '83 will weigh about 500 pounds less than the '82 thanks to extensive use of lighter, stronger materials and new technology.

There's more room in the cockpit, still designed for two lucky people, who sit on newly designed reclining seats. An opening rear hatch makes the luggage compartment truly functional for the first time. Outward visibility is vastly improved with a taller greenhouse and more glass area.

New upholstery, trim, and colors are featured. Instrumentation is by a futuristic vacuum-fluorescent digital-readout display.

The '83 Corvette is about 10 inches shorter than the '82, and weighs some 620 pounds less than the '80 model. Overall, the '83 is lower and shorter, though width is about the same as before. The look is lighter and more European. There's a faint resemblance to the Mazda RX-7 (indeed, CONSUMER GUIDE® magazine predicted the similarity with striking accuracy more than a year before any details were announced) but the 'Vette retains its more muscular appearance. The characteristic front fender bulges are greatly reduced in size, but there's just enough of a hint of them to remind one that this is, indeed, a Corvette.

The windshield appears to wrap fully around to the side glass because of "hidden" A-pillars. The nose and front fenders are combined into a single unit that's hinged at the front and tilts up for superb engine access a la Triumph Spitfire. The previous T-top roof with its twin lift-off panels gives way to a targa-style design and a single removable roof panel that can be stored in a protective bag in the luggage area.

So, the '83 is leaner, lighter, tighter, easier to drive, more economical, and loaded with exciting innovations. 'Vette buffs may recoil at the projected price, however. In 1980 the car's expected retail price was pegged at $21,500. Now, it wouldn't be surprising if the tag read $25,000 when the car is launched in

Inset, above and right: Vega-powered XP-898 of 1973 was rumored as late as 1981 to be the shape of the "next Corvette." The '83 will be vaguely similar in its roofline (opposite page). Below: Comparison of the '83 (shaded area) with the '82 (outline) shows the new model's dramatically lower front end and marked wedge profile. L-83 V-8 will sit far back in chassis.

December of 1982.

The '83 Corvette is a departure from the long-running style that marked the fifth-generation models. In the Corvette's technical history 1983 will join 1956 and 1963 as benchmark years. The '83 is not a classic mid-engine European road car, but it is a highly refined, state-of-the-art sports car in the American idiom. Many believe it will be the Corvette most appropriate for its time. Recalling the '63 and its incredible success makes that hard to believe, but then times *have* changed.

EXPERIMENTAL CORVETTES

"What if" are words that have always started Corvette fans dreaming.

What if GM had produced the

Aerovette? What if the Corvette was redesigned with a turbocharged V-6 and front-wheel drive? What about a mid-engine Corvette? What if the Grand Sport had been produced for the street? Or the Mulsanne? The Mako Shark? The Manta Ray? The Astro II? What if Zora Arkus-Duntov were still watching over the Corvettes of the future?

Hundreds of customizers from coast to coast have taken their personal "What ifs?" and turned their dreams into Corvette realities both stunning and functional.

That's what's been done here, too, as we explored the "What if?" future of the Corvette.

In the following pages, you'll find Corvettes to make your mouth water and your right foot itch. You'll find shapes and sizes you've never seen before. You'll find new ideas

Astro II experimental was shown in late 1967, featured mid-mounted Corvair flat-six.

XP-882 in its original 1970 form. Project was canceled by John Z. DeLorean.

XP-882 featured a transversely mounted V-8 and Toronado-style transaxle arrangement.

XP-987GT was showcase for GM's proposed Wankel engine.

and some ideas that aren't new, but have been translated into the Corvette idiom. These cars are concepts made tangible and alive by the artist's pen. It's very likely you'll find the Corvette of a more distant future among them...only a "What if?" today, but maybe the Corvette of your dreams tomorrow.

Aerovette

Welcome to Fantasyland. What if General Motors decided to put an updated version of the fabulous Aerovette into production? On these pages are just some of the possibilities—and tantalizing they are, too. Before we analyze them, let's recap the history of the Aerovette, one of the most stunning Corvette show cars.

At the New York Auto Show in April 1968, GM displayed a car with the internal code name XP-880, and wearing "Astro II" nameplates. It was really just a styling exercise, constructed under the supervision of Frank Winchell. At the time, many corporate insiders viewed it as a public-reaction trial balloon for a forthcoming mid-engine Corvette. Its drivetrain was a hodgepodge, though it might have been suited for actual production as it was composed of an Oldsmobile Toronado transaxle and other off-the-shelf parts. But it was the styling that excited the enthusiasts. Soon, XP-880 was appearing in full color on car-buff magazine covers all over the country, billed as the "next Corvette."

Meanwhile, crafty Zora Arkus-Duntov was at work on XP-882. This car was definitely engineered with production in mind, since he had created—and patented—a mid-engine chassis layout that allowed the use of stock Corvette and Toronado parts. Mounted just behind the passenger compartment was a big V-8 turned 90 degrees for a transverse location. The transmission was sited under the forward cylinder bank. A chain ran from the crankshaft to a stock

Continued on page 81

GM built two Mako Shark II
show cars — a non-running
mock-up and this working
model (below).

The Aero Coupe (inset) was a
mildly modified production
model that hinted at
changes for 1970 (below).
The big side exhausts and
rear spoiler didn't make it,
though.

At GM, even show cars sometimes get facelifts! The Mulsanne (inset, left) was the Aero Coupe with a new nose and tail that accurately forecast the "crash" bumpers on 1973 (below) and '74 production models. The reshaped front end came first. Note that the '73 pictured is a prototype, and lacks the Corvette emblem.

Horsepower was on the decline in the early '70s as a result of government emissions requirements. The big 454-cid Mark IV vanished after 1974, when it was down from its 1970 high of 465 bhp (gross) to 270 bhp (net). Still, the 'Vette remained one of the fastest cars in the land—and one of the few truly interesting ones, too.

The fifth-generation 'Vette was a decade old by 1977 (below). A retailored roof with a glassy fastback arrived for '78 (right). The 1979 version was mostly a carryover.

Corvette entered the '80s with numerous subtle changes aimed at greater fuel efficiency. A restyled "shovel" nose with integral spoiler appeared for 1980, followed by more extensive use of lighter-weight materials—including a fiberglass-reinforced rear leaf spring—for '81 (opposite top and inset). The emphasis on grand touring luxury (right) continued, with such standards as air conditioning and AM/FM stereo. Meanwhile, a brand-new Corvette was nearing completion, part of which—the drivetrain—was introduced on the '82 (below). It featured a "Cross-Fire" fuel injection system and a four-speed overdrive automatic transmission. Weight was down several hundred pounds from the 1980 model's. Horsepower went up to 200 (net).

To commemorate the last of the "big" 'Vettes, Chevy offered the special Collector Edition model for '82 (below), with lift-up glass hatch and unique paint and interior trim. After some 30 years in St. Louis, production was

transferred to a new,
highly automated plant in
Bowling Green, Kentucky for
'82 (above and upper left) in
an attempt to correct the
Corvette's reputation for
indifferent fit and finish.

Billed as "the Corvette to covet," the 1982 Collector Edition represents the ultimate development of the durable, 14-year-old fifth-generation design. Besides its hatch backlight, it can be identified by special bronze-tinted glass roof panels and cloisonné insignia front and rear. The bold turbine-spoke aluminum wheels hark back to the cast-aluminum wheels of the '63 Sting Ray. The form-fitting bucket seats are covered with multi-tone leather to complement the silver-beige metallic door panels and instrument panel. Each Collector Edition has its own special vehicle identification number plate to prevent someone from turning a standard model into one of these very exclusive 'Vettes.

The long-awaited new Corvette for 1983 will look very much like our artist's rendering (below). The "mirror-image" sketch (left) reveals some similarity in overall size and line with Pininfarina's Ferrari Berlinetta Boxer, but GM stylists have skillfully preserved recognizeably Corvette themes and a definite "American" look. Significant body features (upper left) include one-piece hood-and-fender assembly that tilts forward on gas struts and "targa" style roof with lift up hatch window.

Concealed A-pillars give the "greenhouse" a light, almost delicate look, which contrasts with the husky lower body. The 'Vette's familiar front fender bulges are still evident, but very toned down. New styling should have better aerodynamics than previous models thanks to the deeply skirted bodysides, low nose with integral lip spoiler, and upswept tail. The '83 will weigh several hundred pounds less than recent Corvettes, but won't be that much lighter or smaller overall. The "hi-tech" interior will feature digital instruments.

A collection of mid-engine Corvette show cars. All were touted at one time as possible successors to the 1968 design. The curvaceous Aerovette (center) came closest to production. It was approved for 1980, and made it as far as the clay-model stage. It didn't materialize, though, probably because of GM's need to accelerate its family-car downsizing program.

Zora Arkus-Duntov devised a clever transaxle for XP-882, shown (upper right) as it appeared at the 1970 New York Auto Show. XP-987GT (lower right) was a Pininfarina-built showcase for GM's experimental two-rotor Wankel engine in 1973. It was a companion to the Aerovette, which in its original form was powered by a four-rotor version of GM's stillborn rotary. Astro II (far right) was one of GM's early mid-engine studies. Known as project XP-880, it caused quite a stir among 'Vette fans in 1967, but was never seriously considered for production.

CHEVROLET CORVETTE

Bradley 7.29.80

Here's a look at possible Corvettes of tomorrow. Super-slick model (above) has a number of aerodynamic aids, including twin rear stabilizer fins made of ultra-thin glass and a fully enclosed underbody. Equally striking is the "front" mid-engine proposal (below) designed around a compact turbocharged V-6. Note the race-car-width tires and low, jutting nose.

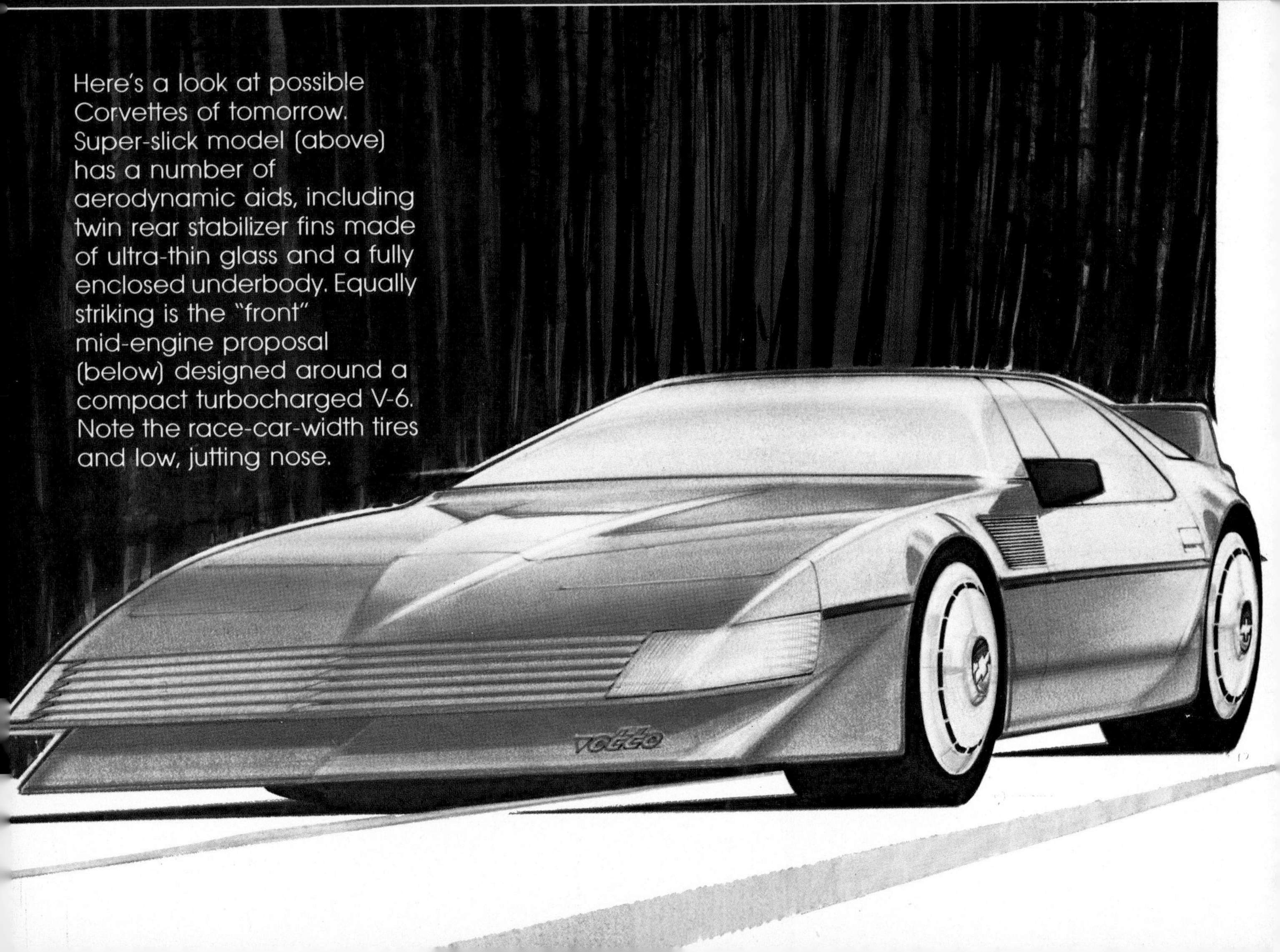

Continued from page 64

Corvette differential through a short driveshaft that turned a 90-degree corner, lined up with the transmission, and then passed through the engine sump encased in a tube.

Two XP-882 chassis were built before Chevrolet's new general manager, John Z. DeLorean, canceled the project. A year later, after Ford had introduced the mid-engine DeTomaso Pantera, DeLorean hauled out the XP-882. Before long it was being used under Duntov's guidance as a test bed for development of GM's then-experimental Wankel rotary engine. Two chassis were fitted with the rotary. The first car had a two-rotor unit, the second a pair of two-rotor engines combined as a single block, to form a four-rotor, 420-bhp engine. Body design was a real headache. As the result of an internal dispute, GM stylists Vinnie Kay and Jerry Palmer were ultimately tapped to draw the lines of the four-rotor car, though the basic shape was conceived by chief designer William L. Mitchell (the two-rotor exercise was done by Pininfarina of Italy). Both cars were first shown in 1973. After the Arab oil embargo hit and the "energy crisis" was on, the rotary's reputation for excessive fuel consumption forced GM to shelve the XP-882 again.

In 1977, however, the four-rotor car was taken off the shelf. Its Wankel engine was replaced by a 400-cid small-block V-8, but retained Duntov's driveshaft-in-sump arrangement. The car was renamed Aerovette and toured the auto show circuit for a time. Actual production, however, remained only a remote possibility.

But Bill Mitchell is nothing if not persistent. He started lobbying at Chevrolet Division for the Aerovette to be the next Corvette. As usual, if Mitchell wanted something badly enough, he got it, and GM chairman Thomas Murphy actually approved the idea for the 1980 program. Ironically, that came about at least partly because of a

The four-rotor experimental became the Aerovette through a simple engine transplant.

Aerovette's snug cockpit housed most minor controls on the center console.

Seen as the next Corvette, the Aerovette design almost made production.

Curvaceous Aerovette was nearly symmetrical front to back and top to bottom.

possible threat from another, soon-to-be-announced sports car — the rear-engine DMC, an independent effort headed by none other than John Z. DeLorean.

By the end of 1977, Aerovette clays were complete, and tooling was scheduled to begin. So for a moment, at least, GM honestly intended to build the car. The production version would have had the same gorgeous styling and a steel platform frame like that of the XP-882, complete with Duntov's clever transverse V-8. The production Corvette engine was a 350 by then, so that's probably the one that would have been used, though it could have been the 305 unit that wound up in California-bound 1980 versions of the existing Stingray. There would have been a choice of 4-speed manual or Turbo Hydra-matic transmissions. The suspension would have been pulled right off the Stingray, which, of course, was Duntov's original, cost-cutting goal. With a fiberglass body, gullwing doors, and fixed side windows, the Aerovette really wouldn't have been any more expensive to build than the Stingray. That would have meant a 1980 price tag in the $15,000-$18,000 range. But with the departure of Duntov, former division head Edward N. Cole, and chief stylist Mitchell, it never had a chance of reaching production.

If any car would have been an instant classic the day it was released, the mid-engine Aerovette was it. Like the Stingray, it would almost certainly have been a 10-year-plus model, one that would have lasted up to 1990 in high style. It's a shame it never materialized. Even so, many of its design principles definitely figure in the 1983 Corvette. And in that sense, Aerovette really *was* the "Corvette of the future."

Aerovette II

In the opinion of many, the Aerovette was the most beautiful car Chevrolet ever created. With a drag coefficient (Cd) of only .325, its shape is one of the most

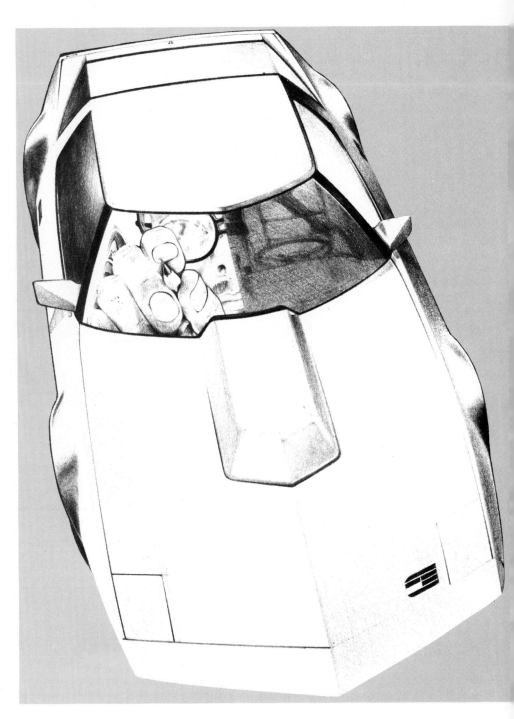

aerodynamically efficient ever devised. Indeed, few all-out dream cars have been as slippery as the Aerovette. Here we take this stunning design ahead by at least a generation in two updated versions of it.

The original Aerovette had a long, sloping tail, and was almost symmetrical above and below the beltline. In the renderings shown, there's less rear overhang, and the

pointed look of the original is gone, replaced by a taut, businesslike tail and spoiler. Note how the rear fenders have been raised. The rear glass hatch is a one-piece unit without lifting struts. The glass is the hot-wire bent type found on the 1977-79 full-size Chevrolet coupes. The nose is shorter than the Aerovette's, with a flatter hood and large, square pop-up headlights. The original Aerovette's windshield wipers were clearly visible. Here, they're hidden under a vacuum-operated pop-open panel as on 1968 production Corvettes.

Side glass is flush-mounted and fixed. Small pivoting front vent windows are provided so the driver can reach out or talk to someone outside the car window without opening the doors. The vents also assist fresh-air ventilation, although the car is equipped with full-time air conditioning.

The front air dam and rear spoiler are rubber trimmed for impact protection. More importantly, they are designed to change their "trim" attitude as speed increases and air pressure rises, thus providing progressively better aerodynamics. The front and rear side markers incorporate cornering lamps for better visibility in turns and extra nighttime illumination for roadside emergencies.

The Aerovette's front fender bulges are deemphasized on our version to create a cleaner, sharper wedge profile. The scoops have been moved above the mid-body breakline. The gullwing-type doors of the original are retained. The Aerovette's sides dropped off sharply below the breakline, but our version features a flatter, slab-sided look. Instead of the original's inverted-U wheel openings, our car has round ones with slightly flared fender lips. While the Aerovette appeared almost grille-less from the front, this update features a black, horizontal-bar grille anchored by huge driving lights and a prominent, low-slung air dam or spoiler.

Like the original, "Aerovette II" is a striking, functional form, and would surely be an eye-catcher. Also like the original, it looks good from any angle. Although the rear no longer mirrors the front and we've

With its inherently good aerodynamics, the Aerovette would have been a natural for racing. Above: A smooth "organic" shape (upper) could be easily "trimmed" for the track (lower) by devices like a full-perimeter skirt and roof-mounted stabilizer wing. Big "flamethrower" driving lights flank the low, twin-venturi grille. Right: Ground-effect skirt and wing's dihedral shape are dramatically evident here.

simplified some curves, the car retains the delicate transitions, the organic flow of lines and shadows, and the air penetration potential of the original.

Competition Aerovette

Corvette's competition record is impressive and well-established. Beginning in 1955 with a record time in class for the Pike's Peak Hill Climb, Corvettes have stormed to victory in all types of racing. Through 1980, Corvettes had won more than 80 significant contests around the world. It's natural that any Corvette wish list would include competition-car possibilities, and that's just what this car is about. The dream racer you see here is patterned after the Aerovette, with some subtle—yet important—updating.

Let's begin at the front. A ground-effect nose and flush-fitting, lay-back headlights *a la* Porsche 928 have been incorporated to trim air resistance and reduce the coefficient of drag. Note also the low hood and aerodynamic windshield. Moving alongside the car, we see wide fender flares, which extend downwards to form a "running board" along the rocker panel area. Note the size of the side air scoop and the aerodynamic paneling from the doorpost rearward. At the rear is a wing supported by fin-like struts. Like the successful Porsche twin-turbo racers, our car sits with a nose-down attitude, the front lower than the rear, for better air penetration and increased stability at speed. The nose bears a resemblance to the GT challenge Corvette campaigned by John Greenwood during the late 1970s, with the exception of the recessed, visible headlamps. The rear wing is similar to the one carried on the car that won the International Motor Sports Association (IMSA) All-American GT manufacturer's award in 1978.

Overall, the design bears a

strong resemblance to the Chevrolet Monza GT show car, which ex-GM styling chief Bill Mitchell has described as one of the most aerodynamic cars ever built. The GT outperformed the contemporary fuel-injected Corvette because it weighed only 1500 pounds. It had hidden instead of recessed headlights, a similar low-drag windshield contour, and an elegant, distinctive body built low to the ground. But our design is sleeker, meaner-looking, and would have tremendous potential as a factory racing car. It is at least as pretty as the racing Stingray and appears considerably more slippery.

In fact, our version was drawn specifically for FIA prototype-class endurance racing. While a racer patterned after the original Aerovette would be too big and heavy for such events, our lighter, smaller version would be admirably suited for, say, LeMans.

If General Motors returned to the track in pursuit of new technology (as foreign automakers like Porsche and BMW have already done) this Corvette could be the car to do it with. If GM's test bed looked anything like our version, it would be a worthy successor to the Corvettes that have earned an enviable record in the fiercest of international competition.

Turbocharged V-6 Corvette

The possibility of a very small Corvette with a turbocharged V-6 engine has tantalized enthusiasts for years. Here we present what could be the pocket-rocket of the future — a targa-topped, low-nosed, high-tailed two-seater with low-profile tires and neat, functional side vents. Powered by a turbo V-6 mounted transversely and driving the front wheels, this sleek little scooter could be

America's answer to the popular Fiat X1/9.

While the side profile is similar to the Italian car's, the three-quarter view shows a quite different contour reminiscent of the Camaro and with an emphasized sense of purpose. The low beltline draws the eye downward, thus enhancing the car's ground-hugging appearance. Fitted with distinctive wheels and low-profile P7-type tires, the car would have exceptional cornering capabilities.

As envisioned here, the "Turbo Six" would have a low, swoopy nose and a high, short back in X1/9 fashion. At the front there are wraparound turn signal/parking lamps, concealed headlights, an air dam, and a lean-back grille. Doors are cut into the roof for easier entry/exit, and flush glass is used for clean airflow.

It's difficult to see too far ahead into the Corvette's future. With inflation, rising gas prices, escalating production costs, continuing government regulation, and all the other headaches, few within the company are willing to predict where the Corvette will go after the 1983 model year. But turbocharged V-6s are being used in GM products now, and it would not be surprising, Detroit-watchers say, to see Corvette carrying such an engine by the mid-1980s. If GM needs encouragement, there could hardly be a more logical body/chassis configuration than the one presented here.

Mid-Engine Berlinetta

One of the most mouth-watering "what if's?" ever to wear the Corvette emblem is our concept of a Corvette designed around a turbocharged V-6 mounted amidships. If you're a car buff, you'll immediately recognize the design influence of one of Italy's fleetest sporting vehicles, the Ferrari 308GTB. But this is more than just a reworked Ferrari.

Notice that the tail has a pronounced Corvette-like appearance enhanced by the lift-up glass hatch, which serves as a cover for the engine

Below: Svelte mid-engine Berlinetta uses a full-width louvered hood intake instead of a conventional grille. Wipers and headlamps are hidden. Far right: Ferrari BB influence is most evident at the rear. Sidewinder V-6 is reached through lift-up glass hatch.

compartment. The nose is clean, with thin, closely spaced slats or louvers for a grille, and a pronounced air dam set at a relatively steep angle. At the base of the flush-fitting windshield are concealed wipers (the Ferrari's wipers are exposed), and the fenders hold pop-up headlamps backed by louvers cut into the fenders. While the Ferrari has teardrop-shaped side vents, this car has more squared intakes. The wheel flares have a sculptured look that adds a sense of balance

and grace to the car's overall proportions.

The rear-end treatment here is interesting, too. Just behind the engine, as in Fiat's X1/9 for example, is a small storage compartment separated from the engine bay by an insulated bulkhead. The insulation is necessary to keep engine heat from cooking anything stored there.

While turbocharging, either by single or twin blowers, would clearly yield a pronounced

improvement in the Corvette's performance, GM has been reluctant to take the plunge. Zora Arkus-Duntov said he asked management to approve a turbocharged L-82 on two occasions: "Each time I was turned down. They say a turbocharged L-82 would sell maybe 1000 units per year. I say more like 6000. But they say it would be unprofitable, and that's the end of the turbocharger for Corvette." It's interesting that Duntov recently lent his name to a turbo

Corvette conversion.

Several specialty firms are now turning out Corvettes with turbocharged 350 engines. Among them is Bob Schuller of California, a veteran Corvette customizer who builds the Duntov Turbo convertible. Schuller's cars come with Goodyear Wingfoot tires and a turbo system of Schuller's own design. It features twin electric fuel pumps and water injection to counteract heat buildup under boost. Schuller also completely revamps the stock Corvette interior, grafts on a massive rear spoiler, and adds a hood air scoop for better engine cooling.

But the days of the 350 are numbered. Former GM President Elliott M. "Pete" Estes said as much in the summer of 1980. All the firm's future engines, he said, will average 31 mpg by 1985, and 95 percent of them are projected to yield 30 mpg city/highway mileage ratings in EPA tests. Interestingly, all will be V-6 spinoffs.

Above and top: A variation on the mid-engine theme is this 2+2 inspired by Ferrari's Mondial V-8. Left: Unique mastaba (truncated pyramid) profile is echoed in wheel housing shape.

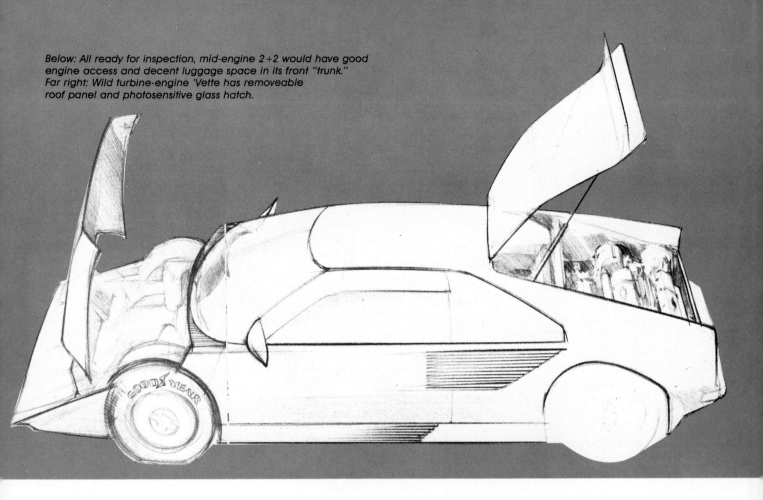

Estes also hinted at the fate of the V-8: "By 1985...20 percent [of GM's engines]...will be diesel...60 percent four-cylinder gas engines ...19 percent V-6 engines...and less than one percent V-8s...In fact, they [V-8s]...probably will be gone by the time we get to 1985." Remove the V-8 from the picture and it appears at least some of that "19 percent V-6 engines" will wind up in future Corvettes. Add a turbocharger to a new chassis and body design and you're getting close to what we present here.

The mid-engine configuration, of course, would be a first for a General Motors production model. Although the company's first serious mid-engine design proposal was drafted more than 13 years ago—in 1967, for the XP-880 Astro II—nothing much has been done with this layout since. Asked whether Chevrolet is seriously contemplating a mid-engine Corvette, GM insiders alternate between belly laughs and chuckles, with comments ranging

from "That's for European cars," to, "Where would you put your luggage?"

The answer, it seems, is that there are no firm plans at this time for a mid-engine Corvette. A pity. The design shown here could be a world-beater.

Turbine Corvette

Ready to let your imagination run wild? Late in 1979, a California Corvette admirer named Vince Granatelli (Andy's son) decided to build a turbine-powered Corvette. The car he came up with will go from 0 to 85 mph in 5.5 seconds, and will run on "anything— kerosene, gasoline, alcohol, even ladies' perfume." It is, as one enthusiast magazine titled it, "The Wildest Corvette in the Whole

Wide World." Here is a prospective turbine-engine 'Vette with the same type of aerodynamic styling that marks all our Corvettes of the future.

The car has a full-width pop-up light bar at the front. The sculptured hood flows back from it to a trio of wastegates at the base of the sharply raked windshield. Our car is equipped with a removable glass panel on top, and a photosensitive glass hatch. The glass lightens or darkens according to ambient light intensity for interior shading— a nifty idea. Our car also envisions a special fiberglass body of great inherent strength and low weight.

This future Corvette could handle the same kind of turbine engine as in the Granatelli car. Fuel is pumped by a Bendix fuel control unit. The driven portion of the engine revolves under full power at an incredible 33,000 rpm. However, revs are reduced through a single-stage epicyclic gearbox to only 6230 rpm at the driveshaft. The car's

power-to-weight ratio is 3.86 lbs/hp for super acceleration up to a top speed of 180 mph. To top it all, the turbine engine weighs only 260 pounds including all plumbing.

The real potential of the turbine engine for future cars rests in its ability to run quite literally on anything, with little effect on performance. But Detroit's attention these days seems focused on electricity; little is said about the turbine. Regardless, this styling exercise demonstrates what could be done if a manufacturer was moved to do it.

Of course, there's nothing new about gas turbine engines for land vehicles. The turbine evolved from reciprocating and radial engine configurations, and really came into its own as an aviation power source during World War II. Although turbine-powered experimental cars have been built since then by such makers as Rover, Fiat, Chrysler, and Renault (not to mention the Howmet Le Mans racer of the late '60s), there

are a considerable number of problems to be overcome before the turbine engine is practical for mass production. In a car, operating speed and load vary constantly, so the turbine's high thermal efficiency, achieved at near peak rpm, can't be realized. The turbine is also thirsty at low speeds, and responds slowly to power demands. Once at or near full power, however, the turbine can be an incredibly efficient means of propulsion.

There are those who believe there is a future for turbine-powered cars. They point to exercises like British Leyland's 25/350/R, a powerplant that develops almost 400 bhp, weighs half what a regular gasoline or diesel engine would weigh, and has a life expectancy of 12,000 hours or about 600,000 miles of average use. But the problems inherent in long-term vehicle use by ordinary drivers make the prospect of a turbine-powered production car very remote.

Electric Corvette 2001

Corvette owners have always gotten a charge out of their cars, but with this one they'll put a charge in. Electric vehicles are definitely part of our future, and sooner or later one of them will be called Corvette.

The search for alternatives to the internal combustion gasoline engine has taken manufacturers, General Motors particularly, to battery power. In the summer of 1980, former GM President Elliott M. "Pete" Estes said the company would definitely build small electric cars. The clay model he showed to the news media fits closely the possible Corvette Electric you see here.

Estes said great emphasis is being placed on aerodynamics, since slippery shapes are even more important for electrics than

The idea of a battery powered Corvette may sound ludicrous today, but technological advances could make it a reality by the end of the century. The overall shape is almost pure wedge for super-low air drag. Bodysides flare out to enclose the wheels fully. Cockpit glass shape and lower full-perimeter skirt recall the Ferrari Modulo show car.

for fuel-powered cars. The power source for the new-generation electrics will be either zinc-nickel-oxide or zinc-chloride batteries. The former has already been installed in a Chevette for testing purposes. In fact, GM has been testing various electrically powered "city cars" for years.

During the '70s, a lot of money was spent on research and development of more powerful, longer-lasting power sources than the ones previously available to the small number of overseas manufacturers already building electrics. Gulf and Western, GM, and others have worked to perfect new batteries that would make long-distance driving practical. With the original Arab oil embargo of 1973 and the resulting dramatic rise in the cost of gasoline, electric vehicle research became more of a priority than ever. GM's announced commitment to put 100,000 electric cars on the roads by the late '80s or early '90s is vivid

evidence that plug-in power may well be the primary alternative to fossil fuel in the coming years. That's why we've included this particular Corvette of the future.

It appears to be an absolute aerodynamic wedge, with covered wheels and a full-skirt spoiler that wraps around the entire car. The rear end is quite similar to that of GM's clay model, as is the door window shape.

If, indeed, the Corvette of the year 2001 has an electric propulsion system, what sort of performance would it have? Let's take today's technology and extend it a little. The sleek Electric 'Vette would slip through the air like few cars today. Its zinc-nickel-oxide battery power system is so intensely developed that the car can reach double the national speed limit of 45 mph. It will run from 0 to 30 in 6.5 seconds, and from 0 to 60 mph in 10.9 seconds. Its digital speedometer will incorporate an automatic power cutoff at 70

mph, but inventive Corvette owners will find a way around that, so they can drive their cars to their 90-mph maximum. Unfortunately, reaching that speed will consume all available battery power because power consumption *triples* from 45 to 90 mph, despite the car's aerodynamic shape.

The battery will be able to sustain a charge for 5 days, the average work week, so that recharging can be done on weekends. If you autocross your Electric Corvette and want to get to work on Monday, you'll have to charge your batteries on Saturday and again on Sunday night. Maximum battery range will be 200 miles; more likely, it would be 140 to 150 miles. Air-conditioner use will be mandatory (the passenger compartment is completely closed) as it is operated by means of temperature sensors.

Sound far out? You bet it does— just like the idea of a Corvette without a big-block V-8 did just a few short years ago.

Postscript

Is there a Corvette of the future? Very definitely. The thoroughly redesigned 1983 model is nearing production reality at this writing. And it promises to be the most roadable, the most exciting, the most rational Corvette since the Sting Ray stunned the automotive world back in 1963.

As for the years ahead, it seems clear from currently available information that the "sixth-generation" Corvette will have a long life—perhaps as long as the 14-year run of the 1968 design. There's no doubt about Chevrolet's commitment to sporting machinery. The smaller, more economical 1982 Camaro is evidence of that. It, too, is a car that's right for the times, yet possesses the spirit, the get-up-and-go, the sheer sex appeal that Detroit seemed to forget in the energy-conscious '70s. Good fuel mileage and low exhaust emission levels are still rightfully important national concerns. But they no longer seem the barriers they once were for stylists and engineers. It's taken a few years, but the industry has at last learned how to combine efficiency and excitement in the same package. The 1983 Corvette certainly reflects post-energy crisis design progess.

In announcing the 1982 Chevy line to the press, division general manager Robert Lund said Chevy is out to put the fun and romance back into owning and driving a car. Surely, the 1983 Corvette is a big part of that effort. In fact, Corvette has never strayed from a simple concept: a specialty car designed for driving and having fun. Is the '83 practical? Not any more than previous models, really. Thrifty? Not like a mundane "econobox" perhaps, but not the gas guzzler Corvettes used to be. Quick? You bet. Able to corner with the best premium-price exotics made anywhere in the world? Naturally.

But what happens after 1983? It's logical to assume the car will change relatively little until it's time for the next full redesign. And right now, nobody—including GM insiders—really knows when that might be needed. In the meantime, the 1983 model should evolve in the same way as its predecessor—minor year-to-year changes mostly to drivetrains, interior trim, and equipment. Engines will certainly become smaller as GM continues to get out of the "V-8 business." But the 'Vette will probably have a fairly large V-8 for at least another five years due to continuing advances in electronic engine management systems that now make this reasonably feasible. A turbocharged V-6, perhaps based on Chevy's 60-degree X-car unit, could materialize as an option in a few years. And you can be sure Chevy engineers will be looking for ways to reduce weight further without resorting to a major downsizing.

Whatever happens to Corvette in the future, it will still be America's premier sports car—its *only* sports car for 30 years. Corvettes of the future may not always measure up to Corvettes of the past, at least in our memories. But there will always be the dreams and the "what ifs?" and books like this one to make our mouths water and our right feet itch for the accelerator. What has been true yesterday is true today and will be true tomorrow: though the car itself may change, the Corvette mystique will endure.